"From the first pag[...] [...]nce to understand grief and the heart to share [...] [...]ith those who are going through it. With honesty and sensitivity, each devotion addresses the real hurt of losing someone we love. Readers will feel not only understood and affirmed, but also challenged to take baby steps and giant leaps towards recovery. Tender, transparent and even humorous at times, Dawn is a great companion on the road to healing."

- HEIDI JOHNSON
Pastor of Care Ministries
Community Presbyterian Church
Danville, California

"Written with compassion by one who has been there, *From Grief to Grace*, is an incredibly helpful devotional for those walking the path of loss. Dawn's style of writing is very relatable as she reveals God's deep and abiding companionship with us as we go through our unique journey. In each devotion, Dawn brings the truth and comfort of Scripture to bear on the tender realities of losing a loved one. While she deals with the questions natural to suffering and pain, she also offers practical help on how to navigate the details and challenges that come in the aftermath of the loss as well as thoughtful questions that help the reader ponder and process their experience. As a Marriage and Family Therapist for over thirty years, I would heartily commend this to any of my clients who are coping with the loss of a loved one."

- LAURA TAGGART
Licensed Marriage and Family Therapist
Author of *Making Love Last*

"This book is honest, personal, and captures the experience of grief up close. As Dawn describes in her book, grief can take your breath away with gut-wrenching sorrow and it can also make you cherish the great moments you shared with a loved one. Grief is messy and different for everyone who experiences it. The amount of time that has passed doesn't necessarily indicate how much you've healed. As a fellow sojourner, Dawn reminds us that we are not alone on our journey of grief as she draws us into the arms of our loving God who weeps with us. I highly recommend Dawn's latest devotional book, *From Grief to Grace,* if you're looking for hope and encouragement as well as a path moving forward."

- CATHY BURKHOLDER
Executive Pastor
Community Presbyterian Church
Danville, California

From Grief to Grace:

A 40-Day Devotional on Healing from Loss

Dawn Dailey

ISBN: 9798637592951

Cover photo: Tulips and hyacinths at Keukenhof, The Netherlands, photo © Dawn Dailey.

Author's note: In choosing the cover art, I wanted a photo that would convey the message of hope in the midst of grief. Flowers traditionally have various meanings. To that end, I chose purple hyacinths which signify grief, pink tulips which denote a sense of caring, and yellow tulips which, along with the budding tulips, represent hope.

In loving memory of my parents,

Wayne and Betty Setzer

Acknowledgements

I thank the Lord Jesus for the seed He planted in my heart that has grown into the book you now hold in your hands or see on your screen. I thank God for giving me the ideas, thoughts, and words. I am in awe of His grace as I walk my own path of grief.

I am much indebted to my Editor Extraordinaire, Liz McCall, whose grasp of grammar is greater than mine and whose insights into wording and phrasing make this work much more readable and understandable. Thank you, Liz! You are such a gift to me!

Also, I want to extend many thanks to my readers, for without you, there would be no purpose in writing this book. I pray that as you read the words, take to heart their meaning, and work through the prompts at the end of each day's reading that you will find the healing you seek between the pages of this book.

To God be the glory!

A Note to the Reader

I am glad you are reading this devotional and I pray that through these pages you will find comfort and peace through God's grace to you. I feel privileged to walk this journey with you.

Before we get started, I want to address an issue that often comes up when someone dies. This is the question of whether or not the deceased knew Jesus or said another way, whether they will go to heaven or not.

Shortly after my brother Logan passed away, someone asked me if I thought he was in heaven. Although he didn't talk about his faith much, I knew that he believed in Jesus. I also knew he lived out his faith by always helping those in need. I answered "yes."

But what happens if you are unsure of your loved one's faith in God? Thinking about the possibility that you may not see them in heaven someday can be distressing. Well-intended friends may tell you that you will see your loved one in heaven, not knowing you may be unsure that will be the case.

2 Peter 3:9 says, "The Lord is not slow in keeping his promise, as some understand slowness. Instead he is patient with you, not wanting anyone to perish, but everyone to come to repentance." God wants to have a relationship with every single person. It is not His will that anyone should choose eternity without Him. But because God gives us free will, we choose where we want to spend eternity. God doesn't condemn someone to hell. They choose not to believe in God or to follow Him.

So how do we know with certainty if someone has chosen to place their trust and belief in God? We don't. Only God does. Our job is not to judge our loved one but to place them in God's merciful and gracious hands. 1 Samuel 16:7 says, "The LORD does not look at the things people look at. People look at the outward appearance, but the LORD looks at the heart." God alone knows our loved one's heart. Because God is good and gracious, we can trust Him, and because He is also all-powerful and all-loving, we know He will do anything to keep someone from choosing to spend eternity in hell apart from Him. Trust in His grace and mercy and let His peace comfort you.

Contents

Introduction

Loss comes in various forms and intensities. Indeed, life is full of loss. The most heart-breaking loss of all is losing someone you love. The permanence of losing your loved one through death requires strength to face life without them. We long to arrive at a place where the pain is not so intense, where, even though we still have a hole in our heart, the pain is not so raw. We never "get over" the loss, but it is possible to go on living, in spite of the pain.

Losing one of my two brothers and both my parents in less than seven years placed my feet on an unwelcomed path of grief. Yet God, in His goodness and faithfulness, showed me His love over and over again. It's His strength that carried my weary soul and His peace and grace that comforted my hurting heart.

Between these pages, I offer hope to you. Not just any hope, but a hope that comes from God Himself, through His Word and His Holy Spirit. As you travel your own journey of grief, may you know you are not alone. May God's grace be more than sufficient for you. May you understand God's love for you as you grow from grief to grace. Come, walk a while with me.

Day 1

Dazed and Confused

May your unfailing love be my comfort. Psalm 119:76

Shell-shocked. Stunned. Jolted. These are the feelings that numbed my brain and held hostage any thoughts when I first learned of my brother's sudden death. My mind could not accept the possibility that what I had just heard was true. I did not want to believe it. I was more than a bit dazed.

How was it possible that someone who was the picture of health one minute could be dead the next? What had happened to my brother? He was alive when his wife left for work that day. What happened while she was gone? How long had he lain on the floor before she found him? Had he tried to call for help? Why did he have to be alone? How did he die? And why? I had so many questions but no answers. I was more than a bit confused.

If you've lost a loved one recently, you may be feeling shocked and disoriented. You may be trying to wrap your head around the fact that your loved one is gone. You may have lots of questions and can't find any answers. All of these feelings are normal when you are grieving. Know that ultimately the fog will clear and you will start down the path of healing. It just takes lots of time and patience. Trust that with time you will find healing. In the meantime, be patient with yourself. You walk this journey of grief at your own pace.

God understands your pain. His heart breaks when your heart breaks. Open your wounded and aching heart to His unfailing love for you. He loves you so.

Dear God, my heart is broken, and I feel overwhelmed and perplexed. Guide me through the fog of uncertainty and lead me to a path of healing. Comfort me with Your unfailing love. Wrap Your loving arms around me and hold me tightly through this painful grief-storm. In Jesus' Name, Amen.

From Head to Heart:

- ♥ What were your initial thoughts when you discovered your loved one had died?

- ♥ What other thoughts did you have in those first few days and weeks? Acknowledge these thoughts and be patient with yourself as you come to terms with them.

Day 2

Jesus Weeps With Us

When Jesus saw her weeping, and the Jews who had come along with her also weeping, he was deeply moved in spirit and troubled. "Where have you laid him?" he asked. "Come and see, Lord", they replied. Jesus wept. Then the Jews said, "See how he loved him!" John 11:33-36

Losing someone close to us is heartbreaking. The pain is overwhelming. Sometimes we feel as if no one else truly understands the depth of our anguish.

Martha and Mary are sisters who lost their beloved brother Lazarus. They are distraught, each in their own way. Martha is more cerebral than Mary whose grief is displayed more emotionally. When Jesus arrives at Lazarus' tomb, John 11:35 tells us that "Jesus wept." These two words comprise the shortest verse in the Bible, but perhaps they form one of the most impactful phrases. Jesus weeps openly at the tomb of His dear friend Lazarus. He shares in the grief of Lazarus' sisters as He enters into their mourning. Like Martha and Mary, He also loves Lazarus. Does Jesus weep because of His own sadness at the passing of His friend? Does He weep because He knows how much Martha and Mary are hurting and their pain causes Jesus to cry?

God doesn't just sit back and watch us go through painful circumstances. He comes to us, enters into our heartache, and weeps with us. He empathizes with us because He has experienced sorrow, too. In the midst of our pain, God walks with us. Lamentations 3:22-23 tells us "his compassions never fail. They are new every morning." Know that Jesus understands our distress and has compassion for us. He feels sad as He weeps over us. Jesus travels with you on your journey of grief. You are not alone.

Dear God, I thank You that You are compassionate and understand my sorrow. Help me to reach out to You in my pain and to feel Your loving presence with me as I travel this path of grief. In Jesus' Name, Amen.

From Head to Heart:

- ♥ Why do you think Jesus, knowing He would raise Lazarus from the dead, wept at Lazarus' tomb? Do you believe Jesus is compassionate towards those who mourn?

- ♥ Read Lamentations 3:22-23 and consider its truths.

Day 3

An Altar of Trust

The LORD appeared to Abram and said, "To your offspring, I will give this land." So he built an altar there to the LORD, who had appeared to him. From there he went on toward the hills east of Bethel and pitched his tent, with Bethel on the west and Ai on the east. There he built an altar to the LORD and called on the name of the LORD. Then Abram set out and continued toward the Negev. Genesis 12:7-9

Abram, later renamed Abraham, is called by God to leave his home and all that was familiar to him to travel to a new land. Except for his servants and livestock, only his wife Sarai and his nephew Lot accompanies Abram. He begins his journey in obedience to the Lord without a clear vision of the future and presses forward through many miles and difficulties. Surely Abram expects a bountiful land that would abundantly supply all he and his family need. Instead, he comes to the land of the Canaanites, people who were certainly not open to giving up their land to Abram. He is a stranger in a strange land. How disappointed and weary Abram must have felt. God had promised Abram many descendants who would inherit the land of Canaan. Even before God's promise comes to fruition, Abram builds an altar to God. Instead of getting angry or impatient with God or wallowing in his disappointment, Abram builds this altar to God as a way of saying, "I trust You, Lord, even when I don't know where this journey will take me."

We, too, are on a journey. For those of us who grieve, we are on a path of loss and sorrow, and we don't know where this road will take us. We, like Abram, have to trust that God knows what He is doing. Our altar is a place where we stop and say, "I trust You, Lord, through difficult circumstances to a place of peace and healing."

God Himself comforts Abram with His divine appearance on two occasions in the first nine verses of Genesis 12. When we feel we are strangers in a strange land, when we sojourn through grief, we too are comforted with God's presence as we find Him in His Word and through prayer.

We, like Abram, can thank God in advance for His comfort, His promises, and His faithfulness. Verses like Joshua 1:5 and 1:9 tell us God will be with us wherever we go and will never leave us. We can trust God to be faithful.

Life is a journey into the unknown. Through new and difficult terrain, may we keep our focus on Jesus who faithfully gives us the strength to move forward as He ultimately leads us to hope and healing.

Dear God, I thank You for the example of Abram, who, though he walked through many difficult circumstances, trusted You completely. As I walk along this sorrowful journey, may I trust You to go before me, to lead and guide me, to comfort me, and to always be with me. Help me build an altar in my heart as a sign of my commitment to trust You more and more. Thank you for Your great faithfulness to me. In Jesus' Name, Amen.

From Head to Heart:

- ♥ Will you trust the Lord right now in the midst of your grief journey? Through prayer, tell God you are trusting Him. Visualize giving Him your grief journey to hold in His mighty hands.

- ♥ How will you build an altar to honor God by choosing to trust Him? Perhaps the altar is a physical reminder or maybe it's a visualization of an altar. What does that altar look like?

Day 4

Great Expectations

Blessed are those whose strength is in you, whose hearts are set on pilgrimage. As they pass through the Valley of Baka, they make it a place of springs; the autumn rains also cover it with pools. They go from strength to strength, till each appears before God in Zion. Psalm 84:5-7

Have you ever been surprised by grief, loss, or suffering? I know I have been. I have great expectations that life is supposed to be smooth, comfortable, and problem-free. Even the least snag, not to mention a life-changing event, can throw me into a tailspin.

Perhaps my perspective is skewed and my expectations are unrealistic. Walking through life is often more of a wilderness experience than an oasis. Yet I unrealistically expect a huge oasis with desert on the periphery. As long as I stay in the oasis, I'm safe from the pain and desolation of wastelands. Or so I think.

The inspired writer of Psalm 84 had it right. We are blessed when we find our strength in God. Even when we walk through the Valley of Baka or Weeping, we can still experience an oasis of refreshment there as we draw closer to God. Perhaps the barren lands have a purpose. In times of suffering, we discover that when we draw near to God, He draws near to us. We realize God wants more than anything else to have a close, intimate relationship with us. Oasis living can mask our need for God. Often, desert treks are where we discover Him and where we find the strength to go on our journey from oasis to oasis until we come to see God in heaven.

Life is not oasis living with a few deserts along the way; it's all about wilderness walking dotted with respite oases. In level-setting expectations, you will be less surprised and will uncover the strength you need to venture forward from strength to strength until you see God face to face.

Dear God, thank You for walking with me in both oasis and desert experiences. May I not forget You in the oasis and may I hold tightly to Your hand as I walk through the desert. May I have great expectations, not of problem-free living, but of Your very presence with me. In Jesus' Name, Amen.

From Head to Heart:

♥ How do your expectations of how life is "supposed to be" impact you? What expectations do you have that need to be more realistic?

♥ How can you begin to accept the loss you are experiencing? Do you believe God is with you as you journey through the desert? Read Psalm 84 in its entirety and apply these truths to your life today.

.

Day 5

Brave New World

"For I know the plans I have for you," declares the LORD, "plans to prosper you and not to harm you, plans to give you hope and a future. Then you will call on me and come and pray to me, and I will listen to you. You will seek me and find me when you seek me with all your heart." Jeremiah 29:11-12

We are often anxious when thinking about the future, even during the best of times. After we lose someone close to us, contemplating our future is downright scary. What is the "new norm"? How can we even think about next month or next year when we are struggling to put one foot in front of the other to get through today?

After the memorial service for my brother Logan, I remember thinking, "Whew, I'm glad that's over." But unfortunately, that was only the beginning. It was unbelievingly difficult to come to terms with the fact that Logan was gone. Outside of our family and close friends, everyone else went on with their lives. Life was back to normal for them. How could I pick up where I had left off? My brain couldn't process all that had happened. I walked around in a fog, sometimes searching for a clearing. Other times, I allowed the fog to envelop me. Most of the time, I hoped I would wake up and this pain would have just been a nightmare, that Logan was still alive and life would go on as it had before he passed away.

Unfortunately, this was my new reality. These painful days have become part of me, part of the fabric of my life that God is weaving for His good purposes. As His word says in Jeremiah 29:11, God still has a plan for me. His plan is not to create more hurt, but to provide hope and healing, a future I can look forward to without fear or anxiety. This is a future that is firmly in His strong grip. I don't need to be afraid.

Amidst the foggy landscape in your head and heart, through all the brain-swirls of fear and anxiety, of pain and sorrow, move into your future as you trust God to take care of you. Step out bravely into the new world as you hold on tightly to Jesus' hand.

Dear God, I know You hold my very future in Your strong hands. I trust You to have my good at heart. Help me to walk slowly, but surely, and bravely toward that new future of hope and healing as I cling tightly to Your hand. In Jesus' Name, Amen.

From Head to Heart:

- ♥ Do you trust God with your future? If not, identify what holds you back from trusting God's good plan for you.

- ♥ Will you take life one day at a time, one step at a time, as you move toward that future God promises you, a future of hope and healing? What is one step you can take today toward healing?

Day 6

We Are Not Consumed

I remember my affliction and my wandering, the bitterness and the gall. I well remember them, and my soul is downcast within me. Yet this I call to mind and therefore I have hope: Because of the LORD's great love we are not consumed, for his compassions never fail. They are new every morning; great is your faithfulness. Lamentations 3:19-23

Is your soul downcast within you? Does your grief consume you? Losing a loved one can do that to us. Grief is a dark cloud of gloom that seems to follow us wherever we go. It touches every corner of the soul. It shows up in places where we don't expect it and always in places where we do.

Healing takes time. So much time. We absolutely have to be patient with ourselves and with those around us. In the midst of our grief, we are the walking wounded, trying to cope with life as best we can, but with a gaping hole in our hearts where our loved one once was. You may not believe this right now while your grief is so raw, but this wound will heal enough to be a scar, always sensitive to touch, but not as painful as it is today. The holes in our hearts will still be there, but the pain will not be as intense.

We have to move forward and process our pain so we can be healed. This is what our loved one would want us to do. Pressing forward, not wallowing in our loss as we work through our grief is necessary for healing. While we may have days when we only want to wallow, hopefully those will be fewer as we move toward healing.

Does moving forward mean we don't care about the one we lost? If we show progress in our healing, do we need to feel guilty that we're not grieving as much as we once were? No, of course not. Grief is the realization that our loved one is no longer here. We feel the pain, but we don't need to wallow in it. Grief doesn't have to consume us. Taking care of ourselves and starting on the road to healing is so important. Are we leaving our loved one behind as we move toward hope and healing? No; we carry them in our hearts as we reach for wellness. Take with you those good memories of the one you lost as you begin your new journey to wholeness.

Dear God, I thank You that Your compassion for me never fails. Your mercies toward my hurting heart are new every morning. Help me not to be consumed with my grief, but recognize that it is a tool to bring me to a place of hope and healing, of wellness and wholeness. I trust in Your love and compassion to carry me to the other side of grief, to a place of healing. In Jesus' Name, Amen.

From Head to Heart:

- ♥ Do you feel consumed by your grief? Feeling overwhelmed is normal, especially when grief is new and raw.

- ♥ Do you feel guilty for trying to move forward without your loved one? Do you think your loved one would want you to feel guilty? What are some good memories you have of your loved one that you can hold onto as you move toward healing?

Day 7

Walking in Jesus' Footsteps

Direct my footsteps according to your word. Psalm 119:133

For most of my adult life, I have exercised several times each week. While I've tried different types of exercise over the years, at one time my routine included walking on a treadmill. The side benefit of working out on a treadmill was the time I had to read, pray, and sometimes just reflect while exercising.

During one such time of reflection, I happened to glance down at my feet where the tread meets the front of the treadmill. I really hadn't paid much attention to the treadmill other than to learn how to start and stop it. As I peered down, I noticed that the brand of treadmill was called PaceMaster®. On days when I really didn't feel like exercising but doggedly plodded along on the treadmill anyway, it felt like the treadmill was definitely the master of my paces and I was its slave!

But it got me thinking. Who is the "master" of my paces? Am I? Do I determine my path in life? Or am I tossed about in a sea of circumstances? Or as a professing Christian, am I following in the footsteps of Jesus? Who is the master of my life? Is it me? Or Christ?

When you are grieving, you may feel you've lost your way and are walking around in a state of confusion and despair. If you are aimlessly pacing up and down, maybe it's time to stop for a dose of direction. If you find your footsteps are taking you on a meandering walk through the wilderness, know that God can direct your path. You don't have to walk blindly through trying times alone. If you are not in the habit of reading the Bible, it's never too late. The Book of Psalms is one of my favorites, as the words portray the psalmist in both good times and difficult ones while they point us back to God, our Deliverer. The Gospel of John in the New Testament is another favorite because it portrays a beautiful picture of how personal and loving Jesus is. Like the disciple John who wrote the inspired text, we too can follow in Jesus' footsteps. Just as exercise is good for the body, reading God's Word is good for the soul. And true to His promises, God will direct our path.

Dear God, thank You for Your Holy Word to me through the Bible. Help me to pursue You by reading Your Word. Show me how to follow in Your footsteps every day, even during seasons of grief. Direct me on the path of life, love, and wholeness. In Jesus' Name, Amen.

From Head to Heart:

- ♥ In this season of grief, do your footsteps have direction? It's common to feel as if you are on autopilot, just going through the motions but without feeling "present". What can you do today to find the direction you need? Perhaps for now, it's simply living more mindfully and intentionally as you go through each day.

- ♥ Commit to reading God's Word every day. The Gospel of John is a good place to start if you want to see how compassionately Jesus interacted with the people along His path. The Psalms, particularly Psalms 27, 30, 42, 46, 61, 63, 77, 84, and 91, are soothing balms to the soul penned by inspired writers who understood grief and pain.

Day 8

Holes in Our Hearts

He heals the brokenhearted and binds up their wounds.
Psalm 147:3

On a sunny spring afternoon, armed with my camera, I took a walk in my neighborhood. I love to take photographs, particularly of landscapes. That day, however, I was on a flower photo expedition. I knew there were huge, beautiful roses close by and I was determined to break away from my to-do list and photograph them. As I approached these gorgeous pink roses, I got distracted. There were other flowers climbing the same fence along with these roses; I had never seen this type before. But what really caught my eye wasn't a flower, but a leaf. It wasn't just any leaf. It was a perfectly heart-shaped leaf. Most people would have overlooked this little gem. You see, some insects had had a proverbial field day with this leaf. It was riddled with holes.

Our hearts are like that leaf. Around the edges, our hearts may be perfectly "heart-shaped", just like they are supposed to be, but upon closer inspection, we discover that there are many holes in our hearts. For those of us who grieve, we have a hole in our heart where we held our loved one. Death creates a cavern there. The deeper the loss, the deeper the hole. The more we love, the more we grieve.

Sometimes other life experiences riddle our hearts with holes, too. Some are tiny punctures, little disappointments, not visible to the naked eye. Others are bigger and create gaping holes. We all have broken places in our hearts. To say we don't is to live in denial of our humanity. Life is full of shattered dreams, disappointments, and losses. If you are feeling like you are the only "walking wounded", you are not. Trust me. You are in good company. To be human is to experience loss.

Thankfully, that's not the end of the story. God takes the holes in our hearts and heals them. The Bible says in Psalm 147, verse 3, "He heals the brokenhearted and binds up their wounds." What a visual that verse is! God takes our brokenness and He wraps His loving and healing bandages around our wounds, binding them tightly in His love and grace. We are safe in the Great Physician's mighty hands where we can experience healing and wholeness.

Dear God, I know there are broken places in my heart. There are holes, tiny punctures as well as gaping ones. Wrap your loving arms tightly around me and my wounds and bring me to a place of healing. In Jesus' Name, Amen.

From Head to Heart:

- ♥ Do you feel alone in your grief? It's common to feel alone while everyone else continues on with their normal activities. Find comfort in the fact that every one of us has suffered losses of varying kinds. You are not alone.

- ♥ Trust that God understands the holes in your heart and that He can indeed bind up the wounds, so that over time you can move toward healing.

Day 9

Gracious Words

Gracious words are a honeycomb, sweet to the soul and healing to the bones. Proverbs 16:24

Words have the power to heal and the power to hurt. We can use our words to build others up or to tear them down. The Bible says when we use gracious words, we can bring about healing deep into the lives of others.

What does it mean to use gracious words? According to Dictionary.com, the word *gracious* means kind, courteous, merciful or compassionate. When we use gracious words, we show others the compassion and love of Jesus.

What about words spoken to us? When grieving, we need to hear words of compassion. All too often, though, well-intended words are hurtful or insensitive. It is common for people to feel uncomfortable and awkward around someone who has just lost a loved one. They don't know what to say but feel the need to say something anyway. What comes out of their mouths may cause you pain. Words like "it was his time" or "it was for the best" may be well-intended, but are incredibly insensitive. Even "you'll see them in heaven" rings hollow to those who are grieving. We need words of comfort, words of kindness, and words of mercy. Words like "I'm sorry you are hurting", "I'm here for you", and "I'm praying for you" show love and compassion. "How can I help you?" carries the practical assistance of delicious meals, babysitting, cards, and flowers.

When words hurt us, we can turn to the God of All Comfort who extends His grace and mercy to us. Many of the Psalms speak words of encouragement. Psalm 46:1 says "God is our refuge and strength, an ever-present help in trouble." In Psalm 63:8, we find "I cling to you; your right hand upholds me."

Jesus understands our pain because He lost loved ones, including His friend Lazarus and His friend and cousin, John the Baptist. When those around us don't have the words we need for comfort, turn to Jesus and the Bible. May God whisper words of grace and love to you as you find comfort in Him.

Dear God, I thank You for Your words of comfort to me. I thank you especially for those You have placed in my life who do indeed know how to offer gracious words to me. Help me forgive well-intended people who say words that hurt me and cause me more pain. May I become a person who uses the power of gracious words to help and encourage others. In Jesus' Name, Amen.

From Head to Heart:

- ♥ Read Psalm 46 and Psalm 63. Let God's gracious words cover you in comfort and give you strength.

- ♥ Is there someone you need to forgive for insensitive words spoken to you in your grief? Extend forgiveness in your heart to them today.

Day 10

Broken Teacups

But we have this treasure in jars of clay to show that this all-surpassing power is from God and not from us. We are hard-pressed on every side, but not crushed; perplexed, but not in despair; persecuted, but not abandoned; struck down, but not destroyed. 2 Corinthians 4:7-9

My brothers and I were throwing around a Nerf football. Normally, this would be a good thing, but we were in the living room. And Mom wasn't home. One wrong throw knocked over an antique teacup sitting on top of the piano. I'm not sure which one of us was responsible for the calamitous throw, but we knew we were in big trouble for breaking that precious antique!

As teenagers, instead of confessing the offense, we thought we could fix the teacup so Mom would never know. So I glued the pieces back together. Weeks later, my mother said to us, "Someone broke my teacup." Uh oh. It was so long ago that I can't remember if we confessed or not, but I do remember Mom was not very happy with us. Suffice it to say, we never played Nerf football in the living room again.

Our lives are like that teacup. When we experience loss, we become chipped and cracked. Broken. As we struggle towards healing, we may look mended on the outside, but if you look closely, you'll see the telltale signs of brokenness. Like teacups that have been mended, we're more fragile than we once were. Loss has a tendency to resurrect itself even when you think you're surely healed by now. One curve ball is thrown at us and we become unglued again.

Jesus puts our shattered lives back together as we look to Him for wholeness. His all-surpassing power at work in our lives brings us hope and strength. While our teacup selves won't be completely healed this side of heaven, we can be glued back together in ways that allow us to move forward. Healing will come over time with the grace, mercy, and peace that only our loving Savior can give. Like the teacup, we're repaired, but not ruined. We're still fragile, but not shattered. We're on the mend, usable teacups once more in the service of our King.

Dear God, mend my brokenness as only You can and restore me to a place of wholeness. Use me as a vessel of healing in the lives of others who have also experienced loss. Thank You for Your grace, mercy, and peace. In Jesus' Name, Amen.

From Head to Heart:

- ♥ In what ways do you feel fragile?

- ♥ How can you reach out to someone else who has experienced loss and be a comfort to them?

Day 11

Of Sparrows and Men

Are not two sparrows sold for a penny? Yet not one of them will fall to the ground outside your Father's care. And even the very hairs of your head are all numbered. So don't be afraid; you are worth more than many sparrows. Matthew 10:29-31

Several years ago, after a mass shooting, a clergyman was reported to say, after acknowledging the sadness of the event, that he believed it was God's will that people lost their lives that day. As I listened to him, my heart went out to the victims' families. I was stunned that he could believe this tragedy was actually God's will.

How does a tragic loss line up with God's will? When we lose someone we love, we are left wondering "why". If God is all-powerful, why didn't He prevent this from happening? If He is a loving God, why did He take away our loved one?

We may never completely understand the "because" this side of heaven. But one truth I hold onto is that God cares for you, for me, and for your loved one. No one escapes His attention. He is all-seeing, all-hearing, and all-loving. He sees our distress. He hears our pleas of anguish. He loves us no matter what.

I struggle with the concept that God allows bad things to happen. I absolutely don't believe He *causes* bad things to happen. Yet knowing He is all-powerful tells me that He could prevent accidents, disease, or senseless acts of violence. As I wonder the "why", I cling to the truth that God is good. He is faithful. And He loves me.

In Matthew 10, the Bible says that God cares about the little sparrows, and He even numbers the hairs on our heads. That God cares for me so intimately gives me hope that God loves me and is not caught off-guard by what happens in my life. While evil abounds and disease runs rampant on earth, God's care extends to me and all my circumstances. He knows what will happen before it happens; He is all-knowing and not bound by time. He knows the extent of my life as the number of my days are known to Him. Psalm 139:16 says "all the days ordained for me were written in your book before one of them came to be."

God knows the brevity of our life. He sees. He hears. He loves. He uses events and circumstances to draw us closer to Him. And when our hearts break, His breaks also. No matter what happens, we know that He walks with us. Wherever we go in life, we are not alone.

As you ponder the "why" of your loved one's passing, know that you are not alone. Just as God cares for the tiny sparrow, He cares for you and for your loved one. God is good. God is faithful. And God loves you so.

Dear God, only You know the "because" to my "why's". Help me to trust You more with the "why" as I cling to You. Just as You notice the sparrow, You see my needs, hear my prayers, and know me and love me. Thank You for Your goodness, Your faithfulness, and Your unending love. In Jesus' Name, Amen.

From Head to Heart:

♥ Verbalizing our questions out loud can be the start of healing. What unanswered "why's" do you have? Say them out loud.

♥ How does your perception of God change after reading about His care even for the sparrows? Will you step out to trust Him more with your unanswered questions and heartache, knowing He is good, faithful, and loves you?

Day 12

Trust

Trust in the LORD with all your heart and lean not on your own understanding; in all your ways submit to him, and he will make your paths straight. Proverbs 3:5-6

    Nights are dark. When we grieve, the days seem dark, too. We meander around without seeing where our next step will be. Life doesn't make sense anymore. We have questions but no answers. Sometimes we have questions we don't even know how to articulate. Our brains are in a fog. On some days it's difficult just to think, much less get out of bed.

    Why does God allow bad things to happen to us? There is no easy answer. Perhaps He allows pain and suffering because through those difficult experiences, we learn to trust Him more. The Lord desires us to be in a relationship with

Him. Trusting Him with the painful circumstances of our lives draws us closer to Jesus and into a more intimate relationship with Him.

What does it mean to trust God? According to Dictionary.com, *trust* means to believe, to have confidence in someone, and to hope. Do you believe God is ultimately in control of your life? Do you have confidence in His ability to take care of you? Do you have hope that God will lead you on a path of healing?

Proverbs 3:5-6 tells us to place our trust in God. To lean on His understanding means to rely on His wisdom and on His word to us, the Bible. Seeking Jesus in all we do, in all our ways, enables us to be guided by Him on that direct path to healing. We won't have to wander on a circuitous route in our grief. Jesus takes us by the hand and leads us to wholeness and peace.

Even though our sense of loss is great, God is greater still. Trust Him. Lean on Him. Walk with Him on the path to hope and healing.

Dear God, thank You that You desire to be in an intimate relationship with me. Teach me to trust You more each day, to lean on Your wisdom and Your understanding, and to guide me along Your path to hope and healing. In Jesus' Name, Amen.

From Head to Heart:

- ♥ Hebrews 11:1 says "Now faith is confidence in what we hope for and assurance about what we do not see." Do you have faith in God and in His love for you? If not, what is holding you back? Can you trust Him with your loss?

♥ In faith, reach out to God today. Trust that He loves you and wants a deeper relationship with you. Lean on Him as you traverse your path of grief.

Day 13

Clinging to Hope

I cling to you; your right hand upholds me. Psalm 63:8

We all suffer losses. Sometimes we endure declining health or the loss of a job or a divorce. The death of someone we love is the ultimate loss.

As humans living in a fallen world, we suffer. Jesus says in John 16:33 that in this world we *will* have suffering and loss. Not maybe. Not might have. We *will*. But in that same verse, Jesus says in Him we may have peace. Without the peace and presence of Jesus, hope and healing remain elusive.

On February 17, 2009, I had no idea what the day would hold. When I received the call that my brother had died suddenly, my whole world turned upside down. There had been no warning signs. No chance to say good-bye. He was 48. Logan had a massive heart attack and in a split second, he was gone. He left behind a wife and two daughters, parents, a brother, coworkers, friends. And me, his sister. One day I was talking with him on the phone and the next week, I was attending his memorial service. Words cannot express the depth of my pain.

Grieving is a lonely process. I spent much time over the next few months grieving and pondering the "why's". Thoughts swirled around in my head while my heart ached. I am thankful for several Christian friends who listened to me and were just there for me.

Often in our deepest despair, we wonder where God is. In those times, we feel God has abandoned us. Like the Psalmists who cried out "God, where are you?", we also cry out, only to hear silence in return. But like them, we too can find God in the midst of our pain and loss. By reading His Word, especially the Psalms, we begin to realize that God shows up, just not as we expect. It isn't some sudden happy feeling that lets us know He's there. Rather it's in the silence, in the darkness, where a fleeting glimpse manifests His presence. That tiny peek into His nearness grows the more we read His Word.

My untrusting heart follows my mind's tentative leading until I, too, like the Psalmist, can say "I trust in You, O LORD. In You, I find my strength." Only when I come to the end of myself and realize I can't heal myself on my own strength do I begin to sense His presence and His peace. I come to trust Him more when relying on God is the only thing I can do. As I search for Him as David did in Psalm 63, I cling to Him and He upholds me with His powerful right hand.

Suffering strips away the props upon which we rely. When we cling to God for life itself, we find Him. When our dreams shatter, we realize that trusting God through the pain and loving Him are what matter most of all. Even when our circumstances are unbearable, God bears us up. He sets our feet on higher ground because He loves us.

Allow God to use the pain in your life to draw you closer, into a more intimate walk with the Savior who loves you so much that He suffered loss, too...on a cross for you and for me.

Dear God, I thank You for Your words of comfort and for Your promise of peace in the midst of my pain. Draw me closer to You. May I cling tightly to You as You uphold me. Help me trust You more as You lead me to hope and healing. In Jesus' Name, Amen.

From Head to Heart:

- ♥ While suffering loss, we often feel abandoned by God. Know you are not alone. God loves you more than you know. Turn your heart toward Him. Seek His presence through prayer.

- ♥ Sometimes it feels overwhelming to open our Bibles and read when our hearts are broken. Make the effort today to read Psalm 63. Read it as your own personal words to the Lord.

Day 14

Into Your Hands

Into your hands I commit my spirit; deliver me, LORD, my faithful God. Psalm 31:5

With arms stretched wide and hands nailed to the cross, in His agony "Jesus called out with a loud voice, 'Father, into your hands I commit my spirit.' When he had said this, he breathed his last" (Luke 23:46). In His painful dying, Jesus knew He was no longer in control. He had submitted His will to that of His Father the night before in the Garden of Gethsemane so that God's higher purpose of salvation would be achieved. His last words are full of submission to His loving Father.

Psalm 31 brims with words of sorrow and hope, calamity and trust. Psalm 31 is thought to be written by David when he was fleeing Saul who was trying to kill him. In these twenty-four verses, David demonstrates trust in God in the face of adversity by pouring out his heart to God, lamenting his situation, and crying out to God to rescue him. Although his faith wavers when his strength fails (verse 10), David puts his trust and hope in God to deliver him.

I love the Psalms and I find comfort in reading and meditating over them. The writers of the Psalms reveal their humanity as they honestly view their state of affairs and share their fears with God. We can see their progress from a fearful state to a state of peace, trust, and even contentment. As they lean into God, He sees them through difficult times.

Psalm 31:5, the verse Jesus quotes from the cross, is a verse of relinquishment, of the realization that sometimes our circumstances are overwhelming and beyond our control. Jesus trusts that God the Father is faithful. Making a conscious decision to place our life, including our loss and grief and even our spirit, into the Father's care is an act of submission to a faithful, loving, and sovereign God. If Jesus spoke this prayer in His distress, why shouldn't we do the same?

Skip to verses 14 and 15 to see the result of verse one. When we acknowledge that God is our God and when we give ourselves up to His care, we can confidently echo the words of David and say, "You are my God. My times are in Your hands". Our "times" include the present circumstances, as well as past and future ones. It also includes our very life and spirit. Although God can orchestrate our situations, He is more concerned about our spirit, which is how we connect with God. When we are in tune with God through our spirit, then He can comfort us and live fully present in us. When we trust Him with our life and spirit, we can let go of sorrow and despair and trust that God, in His infinite mercy, goodness, and grace, will hear our cries for help. He will comfort us, heal us, and carry us through to the other side where He will set our feet in "a spacious place" (verse 8).

When our "times" are in God's strong and capable hands, we have God's strength to walk our journey of healing, knowing that He is with us as we go. God is faithful. Psalm 31 closes out with these words of encouragement found in verse 24: "Be strong and take heart, all you who hope in the Lord."

Dear God, may I, too, pray Jesus' prayer that into Your hands I commit my spirit. I praise You for Your faithfulness. I thank You that when I trust You completely, Your Holy Spirit can completely fill me and give me Your strength, peace, and hope. In Jesus' Name, Amen.

From Head to Heart:

♥ Read Psalm 31 by reading it first from David's perspective as he fled from Saul. Then read it from Jesus' view from the cross. Personalize these verses for your own comfort. What verse or verses are the most meaningful to you? Commit them to memory so you can draw on them whenever you need them.

♥ Take the imagery of God's hands and imagine placing your loss, your cares, and your spirit into His hands. Visualize God taking your concerns and covering you with His love, strength, peace, and hope.

Day 15

God's Masterpiece

Yet you, LORD, are our Father. We are the clay, you are the potter; we are all the work of your hand. Isaiah 64:8

Some time ago I visited the beautiful city of Florence, Italy. At the top of my list of things to see was Michelangelo's statue of David. Housed in the Galleria dell'Accademia, David is bigger than life, standing over 14 feet tall and weighing more than 6 tons. As I gazed on this masterpiece in person, I was amazed at the exquisite detail in the carving.

Although Michelangelo is credited for this sculpture, the history of this famous statue began forty years earlier when the massive block of marble was quarried. Two other artists worked on the project, but neither made much progress. Neglected and exposed to the elements for twenty-five years, the chunk of marble was given to Michelangelo to complete.

Chiseling the fine features and life-like detail took him more than two years to finish. At last, this monumental treasure was freed from the stone from whence it was carved.

Sometimes I feel like I'm that large piece of rough-hewn stone, being chiseled and hammered. With each precise cut, I feel the pain of disappointments, loss, and grief. Sometimes, just like the marble that was to become David, I feel abandoned to the elements, circumstances that seem beyond my control.

The Bible says we are the clay and God is the potter. Just as a master craftsman takes a simple lump of clay, stretches it in many directions, and fires it in a kiln, God takes us as we are, growing us as He refines us in the fires of life here on Earth. The problem comes when we, as the clay, don't like being stretched, poked, and prodded. We can't see the end result. This chiseling process of grieving the loss of someone we love is painful, sometimes more than we can bear. Yet chiseling has a purpose. It creates in us the character, the faith, and the strength to endure. It forms us into the beautiful person God wants us to be – whole, healthy, and healed. Just like Michelangelo envisioned his David in marble, God sees us as who we will become one day - His masterpiece, lovingly created by the Master's hand.

Dear God, You are the potter. Help me remember that I am the clay. Give me even a tiny glimpse of the vision You have for me. Bestow in me the strength to endure the chiseling process as You make me into whom You want me to become. In Jesus' Name, Amen.

From Head to Heart:

♥ Take a few moments to think about the analogy of the potter and the clay. In what specific ways do you feel stretched, poked, and prodded as you grieve? Visualize this in terms of clay or marble.

♥ Visualize giving that lump of clay or block of marble up to God. Give your pain to Him. He cares for you so.

Day 16

In a Dry and Parched Land

You, God, are my God, earnestly I seek you; I thirst for you, my whole being longs for you, in a dry and parched land where there is no water...Because you are my help, I sing in the shadow of your wings. Psalm 63: 1, 7

King David was forced to retreat to the desert; when his son Absalom tried to kill him, David fled to the desert in terror. He experienced physical thirst and hunger as he ran for his life. As David longed to meet God in that barren wasteland, his yearning for fellowship with Him was as great as his need for food and water. David knew that only God could satisfy his hunger and quench his thirst, both physically and spiritually. Only God could meet his needs. Only God could save him.

While we may not be in physical danger, we do have emotional losses, broken places in our lives. Sometimes we wander around in our own barren wastelands. Life feels like an arid desert, void of sustenance. Unlike David, however, we may not feel that God can meet our needs or that He is even there. The times when we most need to seek God may be when we least likely feel like finding Him because circumstances overwhelm us. But when we long for Him, when we thirst for Him in a dry and parched land, He hears our hearts' cry.

David even went a step further. Not only did he seek God out in his difficult situation, but he also sang this psalm of praise to God. David acknowledged that God was his sole source of help. He sang praises to God as he rested safely in the shadow of God's wings.

Our throats may feel too parched to sing praises. Our hearts may be too downtrodden. But when we acknowledge that God is still our God, in our desolate landscape we find the beginning of our healing process. When we experience huge losses, like losing someone we love, when the day-to-day gets overwhelming, God delivers on His promises. He is our help and will cover us with His mighty wings.

Dear God, You are my God. I earnestly seek You in a dry and parched land because only You can satisfy my hunger and thirst. You are my help, O God. Enfold me in the shadow of Your wings. In Jesus' Name, Amen.

From Head to Heart:

♥ Read Psalm 63 in its entirety. Let the words seep into your soul. Believe God is your help and that He will uphold you in your grief.

♥ Find a Christian praise song that is meaningful to you and listen to it today.

Day 17

Rose Garden Promises

"In this world you will have trouble. But take heart! I have overcome the world." John 16:33

There's an old song entitled "I Never Promised You a Rose Garden". The lyrics make it clear that life isn't full of roses and sometimes, instead of sunshine, we get rain. The Bible also has a similar verse. In John 16:33, Jesus says that in this life, we will experience suffering. He tells us to be encouraged. He has overcome the world by His victory over death itself.

I wonder how many of us really believe His promise. In the midst of grief, it is all too easy to feel God has deserted us.

But you see, God really does promise us a rose garden. The problem is we expect that garden to be free of thorns. When the thorns tear our souls and cause us pain, do we run to God our healer or do we retreat to our own make-shift bandages? How do we live in the rose garden and deal with those prickly thorns? We do have a choice.

To paraphrase C.S. Lewis, a renowned Christian apologist, God may seem quiet in the good times, but He shouts to us in our pain. Do we hear God shouting His love and mercy to us when we are surrounded by jagged thorns? Are we listening? Do we feel His loving presence? Or do we only see the thorns and ignore the beautiful roses?

In our anguish, we may feel God has left us. Our souls ache. We long for an easier road to travel, a rose garden without thorns. Deuteronomy 13:6 says "Do not be afraid or terrified… for the LORD your God goes with you; he will never leave you nor forsake you." The good news is God has not left us. We may be sad and full of grief so that we don't realize He is there. If we allow Him to lead us, the thorns along the trail are teachable moments for us, chances to draw closer to God and opportunities to see His power manifested in us. Those painful "thorn-filled" moments are the way God shouts His love to us. He cares for us through both the thorns and the roses of our journey. Listen to Him shout His love and care to you amidst the thorns in your life. He loves you so.

Dear God, I claim today Your promise that you are always with me and will never leave me. Teach me Your ways and purposes through the thorns in my life. Fill me with the sweet fragrance of Your rose in the form of Your love and presence. In Jesus' Name, Amen.

From Head to Heart:

♥ Read Deuteronomy 31.6 *(handwritten)* ~~13.6~~. Know that you are not alone, that God goes with you. Trust Him with your fears and grief.

♥ In one of his poems entitled *Endymion*, John Keats said "A thing of beauty is a joy forever". Buy a bouquet of flowers and let it be a reminder of God's love and care for you today.

Day 18

Pursuing Appleseed

How long must I wrestle with my thoughts and day after day have sorrow in my heart?...But I trust in your unfailing love; my heart rejoices in your salvation. I will sing the LORD's praise for he has been good to me. Psalm 13:2, 5-6

Children often sing the "Johnny Appleseed" song about being thankful for God's goodness. Even preschoolers can recite this song as a prayer with tiny hands folded, heads bowed, and voices singing. But do we as much older and wiser grown-ups believe that God is good? Do we thank Him with hearts of gratitude?

In our struggle over loss and death, we wrestle with our thoughts about God's goodness. Sometimes, like David in Psalm 13, we have doubts of God's goodness when we look at our situation. We do wonder when our heartache will end and how long we have to suffer. We may feel like Job where nothing is going right and heartache is at every turn. We miss our loved ones, but nothing can bring them back to the land of the living.

God is with us in the middle of this gut-wrenching despair. He does not leave us alone. Most of all, He desires a relationship with us. He carries us when we're too weak to walk. He never gives up on us because He is good. Just as parents want to give good gifts to their children, so God wants to give us good gifts (see Matthew 7:11). In the midst of our suffering, He gives us the gift of His presence. He pours out on us His gifts of mercy, grace, and peace.

While we don't feel grateful *for* our circumstances, we can begin to feel grateful *in the midst* of them. Not thankful for our loss, but thankful for God's care and comfort *during* our difficult circumstances. When we focus our eyes on the Lord, lifting them way above our situation, then we can see God and His goodness and begin to feel a sense of gratitude.

Can we receive those gifts of mercy, grace, and peace in the midst of our grieving? Can we claim those gifts for our own? Perhaps we don't have the capacity to receive God's gifts right now. Maybe our emotions and grief get in the way. Our inability to receive God's help during our time of sorrow is like a drowning man who is so busy flailing his arms and legs in the water that he cannot grasp the life-preserver thrown to him. Reach for that life-preserver and take God's help. Ask and His gifts will be given to you. When you seek God, you will find Him.

May we, like David, sing God's praises even as we cry out in our sorrow, "How long, O Lord?" Let us turn our wrestling thoughts to the goodness of God, to His great love for us. May His presence and peace fill our minds as His mercy and grace surround our hearts. Let us receive His gifts with gratitude, for He is indeed good.

Dear God, I thank You that You are good. Even in the midst of my sorrow, I remember Your goodness and kindness to me. I thank You for Your gifts to me - Your very presence, Your mercy, grace, and peace. May I give up my wrestling thoughts to You as I receive Your good gifts to me. In Jesus' Name, Amen.

From Head to Heart:

- ♥ Seeing God's goodness when your heart is broken is difficult. While being grateful *for* our circumstances may be impossible, how can you begin to become grateful *in the midst of* them? How can you see God working in your life right now?

- ♥ Know that God loves you and His heart breaks for you. How can you be thankful, not *for* the loss, but *during* this painful time? Allow God to comfort you in your distress. Seek Him in His Word. Read and ponder all verses in Psalm 13.

Day 19

Working Through Anger

You have searched me, LORD, and you know me. You know when I sit and when I rise; you perceive my thoughts from afar. You discern my going out and my lying down; you are familiar with all my ways. Before a word is on my tongue you, LORD, know it completely. Psalm 139:1-4

When I suffer a loss, sometimes I feel angry. I don't understand why God let this happen. He's all-powerful. He could have prevented it, but He chose not to. My fury can escalate into angrier thoughts and accusations towards God. I am my four-year-old self again, throwing a tantrum, not caring who sees.

God sees. Psalm 139 tells us that God knows my thoughts before they are even formed in my mind. He even knows I'm going to get angry before I actually do. But I keep returning to the fact that God is good. And He loves me. He is a good

Father. He doesn't intentionally allow painful events to happen. But He is all-powerful and can use those circumstances for good in my life. Even tragedies can be used to teach me, to draw me closer to the God who loves me more than life itself.

One name for God is "Abba" which means "Daddy". I imagine throwing that tantrum, beating on His chest with my fists, while His loving arms are wrapped around me, tightly holding me until I'm spent. God can handle it. The ability to be completely honest with God about my anger is actually healthy. Perhaps this might look more like anguished prayer, where we're pouring the pain and suffering in our heart out to God. The more we share our feelings with our heavenly Father, the more His loving arms draw us close.

Ephesians 4:26 says, "In your anger do not sin". Being honest with God about our questions, the "why's" of our loved one's passing, and the anguish we feel is good. But take care not to let that anger fester. Pulling away from God because of our anger is unhealthy and wrong. Staying furious with God for months and years hardens our hearts towards Him. Our prolonged anger becomes the knife that severs our relationship with God.

We all experience the "why" questions. We want to know why our loved one died, why their death wasn't prevented, and why more wasn't done to save them. It's okay to question God and to express anger and frustration. He knows our thoughts anyway. But take care not to be angry to the point of sin, where we harden our hearts towards God. He is indeed good. He loves you as a good father.

Dear God, I thank You that You love me enough to allow me to express my anger to You. Help me work through my feelings in a healthy way that doesn't damage the relationships I have with You or with others. Hold me close in my anger and frustration. Give me strength to work through anger and get to a better place. In Jesus' Name, Amen.

From Head to Heart:

- ♥ Read Matthew 14:6-13 where Jesus learns of his friend and cousin John the Baptist's death. Enter into Jesus' sorrow at that moment as you read verse 13.

- ♥ Are you feeling anger or frustration about the death of your loved one? If so, how are you expressing your feelings? Are you being honest with yourself and with God? Set aside some time today to pray, to share your feelings with God, and to experience His love and compassion.

Day 20

Forgiveness

For if you forgive other people when they sin against you, your heavenly Father will also forgive you. But if you do not forgive others their sins, your Father will not forgive your sins. Matthew 6:14-15

Forgiveness is one of the most difficult concepts in the Christian life to understand and practice. In the book of Matthew, Jesus is teaching the disciples how to pray with what we call the Lord's Prayer (see Matthew 6:9-13). Interestingly, Jesus follows up that prayer in the very next verse with an explanation of forgiveness. Perhaps it is because the disciples need to clearly understand how to forgive. So do we.

When someone else has caused or contributed to the death of our loved one, forgiving is the last thing we want to do. Whether their actions were intentional or not, we find it most difficult to forgive them. Even thinking about forgiveness dredges up anger, resentment, bitterness, and even revenge. We replay the circumstances over and over in our minds, cementing the desire in our hearts to never forgive.

Just as cement hardens into concrete, unforgiveness hardens our own hearts. We may believe we are in control or protecting our hearts when we choose not to extend grace to others, we only hurt ourselves. Refusing to forgive is like drinking poison while hoping the other person will die. By not forgiving, we lock ourselves into a prison of our own making. We are the ones who suffer and will continue to suffer.

When someone has caused our loved one's death, it is understandable and even human to not want to forgive them. It is frightening to open ourselves up to forgiveness. We don't want to lose the feeling of anger towards them because that anger creates feelings of power and being in control. The simple truth is we are in control neither of our circumstances nor the actions of others. We can, however, control our responses, our own actions, and yes, even our thoughts.

Contemplating forgiveness steps us back into the raw pain of the loss. Forgiveness scares us because the very thought of forgiving someone makes us feel vulnerable and defenseless. The reality is we are not opening up to the offender. In considering forgiveness, we open ourselves up to God who alone has the power to forgive. When we admit we can't forgive on our own, His power and strength work in our hearts. Like Paul in 2 Corinthians 12:9-10, we can trust in

God's strength, for it is when we are weak that His strength shines through us.

God is ultimately the judge. While we can ruminate on the offender and create our own courtroom in our heads where we are both judge and prosecutor, the sentence falls on our heads, not theirs. God is just and it's His job to judge, not ours. When we turn over the offender to God, He will see that justice is done, either in this life or the next. Letting the offender off the hook doesn't condone their actions. It frees us from the burden of anger, resentment, bitterness, and revenge. When we freely forgive, we can live freely.

In Matthew 6:14-15, Jesus says we are to forgive others so that God will forgive us. Forgiveness really isn't an option. Jesus died on a cross for our sins and yes, even the sins of the offender we don't want to forgive. While some say that forgiveness is a process, I believe that forgiveness is a choice. Healing is the process that begins after we decide to forgive. Getting to that point of forgiveness may take time, but opening our hearts to God who has the power to forgive is the beginning of healing. Living a life undefined by our tragedies is a life lived well, in the freedom and wholeness bestowed by the power of forgiveness.

Dear God, You forgave even the ones who nailed You to the cross. I know that the only person who is hurt when I don't forgive is me. Free me from my prison of unforgiveness as I open myself up to Your loving grace. May I choose to forgive and experience the freedom and healing I need. In Jesus' Name, Amen.

From Head to Heart:

- ♥ Is there someone responsible for the death of your loved one? If so, have you made the decision to forgive? If not, as painful as this may be, what is holding you back?

- ♥ If there is no one responsible for the death of your loved one, is forgiveness still in order? Is there unfinished business with your loved one that you need to let go? Are you impacted by survivor's guilt?

Day 21

Help in Time of Need

I lift up my eyes to the mountains – where does my help come from? My help comes from the LORD, the maker of heaven and earth. Psalm 121:1-2

Details can be overwhelming, can't they? Life is busy and there are so many tasks that vie for our attention. Losing a loved one means there are probably additional tasks that require one's time and effort. Sometimes it is difficult to know where to start. Often our loved ones left things undone. Perhaps we have to figure out how to dispose of their personal belongings. After the funeral or memorial service, where do we begin?

Details come in all shapes and sizes. Perhaps you are struggling with being the executor of their will or making sure all their bills get paid. Maybe they left personal belongings that serve as a constant reminder that they are gone. Putting those items out of sight could be helpful. Perhaps it's time to determine what to do with all of their personal effects.

Combing through all these details can be very emotional. Many memories are associated with belongings. Sorting through their personal items can feel like you are invading their privacy. Tasks like these are difficult to accomplish, especially when alone.

Where do you turn for help? As the writer of Psalm 121 says, "I lift my eyes to the mountains – where does my help come from?" Our help ultimately comes from the Lord. Ask Him for the help you need. Pray He will provide for you and give you the strength you need for the tasks at hand. Ask other people to help you sift through all those personal belongings, to help with paperwork, and even just to be with you as you work on one task at a time.

Even though the mountain may appear foggy right now, God is still there. He is our source of help and strength. Keep looking up to Him as He abundantly provides for your needs.

Dear God, I praise You because You are the maker of heaven and earth. Nothing is beyond Your reach. As I lift up my eyes and heart to You, I pray You will provide me the strength and resources I need to do all the tasks before me. I thank You, in advance, for Your provision. In Jesus' Name, Amen.

From Head to Heart:

- ♥ What tasks at hand need immediate attention? Prioritizing to-do items can help you focus on what's important or urgent.

♥ Who can you reach out to today to help you with the immediate work that needs to be done? Pray for discernment and don't let fear keep you from asking someone to help.

Day 22

A Nostalgic Moment

If any of you lacks wisdom, you should ask God, who gives generously to all without finding fault, and it will be given to you. James 1:5

As I entered the rustic interior, I noticed the hammered copper distillery in the corner, the dark wooden beams in the ceiling juxtaposed against the white-washed walls. I requested a table away from the door. Consequently, I was seated next to a large column. The table felt private and away from curious eyes.

The server was friendly, and after conversing and ordering, I waited for my first course. I glanced around the room again. Set in a tiny French town, the restaurant was full of history. As I looked at the wall next to me, my eyes took in what my heart was slow to grasp. In a large shadow box were almost a dozen white antique baptismal baby caps. Dainty with laced edges, the hats struck a chord deep inside me.

For as long as I can remember, my parents had hung on our living room wall my father's baby bonnet set in a frame. Another frame held a pink quilted heart-shaped keepsake of my mother's infancy. As I stared at the shadow box in this restaurant miles from home, the weight of grief descended upon me. What happened to those two frames belonging to my parents? Did one of my family members have them? Were they sold in the estate sale?

I suddenly felt guilty. Why hadn't I made sure I retrieved those treasures? Perhaps I had felt so overwhelmed by all the belongings my parents, packrats that they were, had left behind that it would have been impossible to keep everything. I could only guess that at the time, these keepsakes were not on my radar screen, that there were other memorabilia I chose to keep instead.

Grief raises its head at the most unexpected moment. Taking in our surroundings and focusing on something that reminds us of our departed loved ones can take us by surprise. Sadness and even guilt can move into our hearts on a moment's notice.

In this particular instance, I had to recognize this was a nostalgic moment. It was okay to feel sad for a few minutes. Guilt, however, was an unwelcomed intruder. Going through my parents' belongings after their deaths, I knew I had done the best I could under the circumstances. I also realized that what had meant a lot to them wasn't as meaningful to me. In order to move forward in my grief, in the land of the living, I had to put aside the tendency to regret, and instead remember with fondness my parents' sense of nostalgia and their good qualities and characteristics.

As the saying goes, "You can't take it with you". Perhaps it is best not to saddle someone else with one's belongings in the first place. But if you find yourself in this situation, pray for God's wisdom while sifting through someone's personal things. Trust in His grace when dealing with guilt. When we pray for wisdom and grace, God will answer our prayer. Always.

Dear God, life is full of decisions to make, especially after we lose someone we love. Please fill my head with Your wisdom and my heart with Your grace. In Jesus' Name, Amen

From Head to Heart:

- ♥ What has triggered your grief lately in unexpected ways? How have you worked through the grief?

- ♥ It's never too late to pray for God's wisdom. If you feel overwhelmed by decisions, stop now and ask for God to fill your mind with His wisdom and your heart with grace. Believe you are doing the best you can.

Day 23

Packrat Tendencies

"Do not store up for yourselves treasures on earth, where moths and vermin destroy, and where thieves break in and steal. But store up for yourselves treasures in heaven, where moths and vermin do not destroy, and where thieves do not break in and steal. For where your treasure is, there your heart will be also." Matthew 6:19-21

I'm the child of a child of the Great Depression. Because they grew up in the 1930's, both my parents couldn't stand to throw anything away. Consequently, closets bulged, the attic overflowed, and the garage was a hazard to walk in. Thinking they "might" need something, they held onto it, often until it was no longer usable.

After my father passed away and my mother moved to a retirement community, we had the arduous task of cleaning out their house. The thought of sorting through years of accumulated stuff was overwhelming. If it weren't for the senior move manager and the "estate lady", I would still be at their house, sitting among piles of stuff. Although I have packrat tendencies myself, even I couldn't fathom why they had saved what they had, moving it from one house to another, during their more than fifty years of marriage. I wished they had cleaned out, even a little bit at a time, making it a practice to only keep what they actually needed. When my mother passed away several years after my dad's death, I was thankful we had already done the monumental task of cleaning out their house. What little she had left was easier to sort through.

On a practical level, if you find yourself in a similar situation, reach out for help from family and friends. It is difficult to sift through a loved one's belongings because everything reminds you of lost loved ones. If possible, enlist the aid of a senior move manager or other professional to comb through your loved one's possessions and help you disposition them.

Grief is like accumulated material goods. We can let grief pile up, or we can periodically sort through it, doing the hard work of cleaning up our grief so it doesn't clutter our lives and cause us to trip further down the road. Particularly if we are dealing with more than one loss, we don't need to let them accumulate until they become overwhelming.

Jesus says, in Matthew 6:19-21, that we are not to store up our earthly treasures, but rather we are to use our earthly treasures for His glory, to further His kingdom's purposes. By investing in His kingdom, both materially and spiritually, our hearts will not become ensnared by the distractions of this world. When we place our trust in God, our desires align with His will and our treasure becomes our relationship with Him.

When we make the effort to healthily sort through our grief, to acknowledge both the losses and our feelings, we can live freer, without the clutter of the past causing roadblocks in our present relationships. When we de-clutter, by working through our grief, not ignoring it, we can be healthy and free to place our real treasure into God's hands. We can trust Him to take care of our spirits when we get to a place where we want God more than we want our material possessions, or even more than our loved ones. In the midst of our grief, we can trust God to carry us through, to be present with us, and to help us as we do the difficult, but necessary, work of grief.

Dear God, help me not accumulate material possessions or emotional losses. Show me the value in storing my treasure in heaven. Help me de-clutter my life and refocus my heart on You. In Jesus' Name, Amen.

From Head to Heart:

♥ Are you dealing with the material possessions left behind by a loved one? How can you enlist the help of family, friends, or professionals so you don't have to sort through it all by yourself?

♥ How are you doing with intentionally working through your grief? Are there losses in the past that are compounded by your current loss? What steps can you take today to sort through your grief?

Day 24

Fearless in the Everyday

The LORD is my light and my salvation – whom shall I fear? The LORD is the stronghold of my life – of whom shall I be afraid? Psalm 27:1-2

Losing someone we love takes us to a lonely place. When we feel alone, it's often difficult to move forward in life. Especially if we've lost a spouse, sometimes making everyday decisions is challenging. But even if our loss is of a different kind, losing others close to us can cloud our thoughts so that our jumbled minds have trouble forming sentences, let alone making decisions.

It's generally considered wise counsel to wait a full year before making any life-altering changes, like moving to a new house. We need time to ensure we're making the right choices for ourselves.

But what about the smaller decisions? When we're used to having someone else to jointly decide with us, the sudden absence makes it impossible to reach a decision. We find ourselves afraid that we'll make the wrong choice without help.

It's easy to feel afraid after losing loved ones. We feel a fear of the future, moving forward in life without them. But there are also the little nagging fears of the everyday that cause life to become murky as we muddle through our grief.

Ralph Waldo Emerson said "always do what you are afraid to do". Obviously, this doesn't mean doing something inherently dangerous, but it does mean facing your fear and doing "it" while afraid. "It" could be making those everyday, household choices without the help of your partner and trusting yourself and God that you will make a good choice.

No matter what our circumstances are, we can, as today's verse says, follow the Lord and not be afraid. Why? Because God is the stronghold of our life. He has built a fortress around us where fear cannot enter. We can trust Him to keep us safe. We don't have to fear even seemingly minor decisions. We can move forward through our fear, knowing God is with us.

Dear God, I praise You and thank You that Your loving arms surround me when I feel afraid. Help me make the choices I need to make today, without fear, knowing You are with me. In Jesus' Name, Amen.

From Head to Heart:

- ♥ What decisions are you making currently or will make in the near future that you feel afraid to make on your own? Are you willing to trust the Lord to be with you in the decision-making process?

- ♥ Can you visualize the stronghold God has built around you? What does it look like? Will you take this visual with you throughout your day?

Day 25

To Sleep, Perchance to Dream

...for he grants sleep to those he loves. Psalm 127:2

Sleep is a precious commodity, especially when one is walking on a journey of grief. Quieting one's mind and heart can be challenging. Feeling rested evades us, and sometimes nighttime can increase our sense of loss and loneliness. Darkness becomes our nemesis. Nightfall morphs into an opportunity for our active minds to dwell on our loss. Spiraling down into a dark abyss is easier at bedtime without all the distractions from the day. When we should be sleeping, our minds are active with "what if's" and "why's".

The Bible tells us that God gives sleep to those He loves. Claim that promise for yourself. Try clearing your mind of your cares and anxieties and cast them all on Jesus, for He cares for you so much (1 Peter 5:7). Believe God will grant you the sleep you need. Then relax your mind and body as you prepare for sleep.

After you wake up, do you remember your dreams? Perhaps there are dreams you'd rather forget. Perhaps you're experiencing nightmares as a result of the trauma of losing someone you love. After a tragedy, it's normal to have bad dreams. It's okay to seek medical attention if the nightmares recur frequently. Sometimes we need help in processing our thoughts when our unconscious mind is overactive.

Other times, we have dreams we wish would last longer, from which we don't wish to awaken. The times I have dreamed about my brother after his death have been pleasant dreams, until I wake up and realize they were just dreams. In those dreams, I know my brother has died and I can only hang on to him for just a little while longer before the dream is over. Dreaming about him is a comfort to me as I walk through this life on earth without him. May you find peace in sweet sleep and may your dreams be pleasant reminders of God's care for you.

Dear God, I come before You as a weary sojourner on this path of grief. Your word tells me that You grant sleep to those you love. May You fulfill that promise to me tonight, to give me restful sleep and pleasant dreams. May I cast all my anxieties on You as I rest in Your comfort and care. In Jesus' Name, Amen.

From Head to Heart:

♥   What thoughts control your mind as you try to sleep at night? Identify the thoughts that disable you. Every time these thoughts pop into your mind, give them up to God in prayer. Then think about what is true, noble, and right (see Philippians 4:8). Sometimes writing down adverse thoughts in a journal will keep you from ruminating over them. Eventually, these negative thoughts will lose their power over you.

♥   If you find relaxing for sleep to be difficult, try using a meditation app with a five- or ten-minute practice session specifically designed for sleep. *Calm* and *Headspace* are helpful meditation apps. *Relaxio* is another app that plays relaxing sounds, like rain or a rushing river.

Day 26

Grief Will Wait

Like a lion in cover he lies in wait. Psalm 10:9

In our instant gratification culture, "waiting" isn't something we like to do. Did you know that the word "wait" appears over 100 times in the Bible? While the Bible often associates "waiting" with "trusting", I'm referring to a different kind of "wait".

Like a lion seeking its prey, the grief enemy stalks us, overtaking us at times with tears and sadness. I have often been surprised by grief and its suddenness. When you've lost a loved one, it doesn't take much to flood our minds and hearts with the fact that someone we love is gone. And it hurts. Very badly.

There are those of us, however, who prefer to remain stoic. Living in denial that we've suffered a loss, we plow on through life. We obliterate the truth that we are hurting.

Others of us acknowledge we feel loss but are unable to process and sort through our feelings.

Here's the bottom line: Grief will wait. Grief will wait for you to come to terms with the fact that you've experienced loss. While it can be postponed, grief will lie in wait until you are ready to deal with the pain. For some of us, that "waiting" may take years. In the meantime, the undercurrent of our loss, perhaps subconsciously, permeates our relationships, like a poison. Not dealing with our loss impacts us to the very core of who we are, sometimes shaping our perceptions of ourselves and our self-esteem.

Here's the hope: Let yourself grieve. For it is in the process of grieving that we truly find ourselves. In the difficult times when we reflect, journal, process, or do whatever it takes to work through our sense of loss, we become stronger and healthier and whole.

Grief isn't the enemy. Denial is. Only when we acknowledge our loss and our need can we begin the journey of healing. Grief brings us closer to the God of All Comfort, the God who loves us more than we can ever hope or imagine. For it is in the darkness that we reach for the light, the light of God's Word for our path (Psalm 119:105) and for Jesus, the Light of the world (John 8:12). Through His healing power, we are made whole. It starts with awareness. Let yourself grieve. Embark on your path of healing today.

Dear God, I thank You that You are the God of All Comfort. I thank You for walking with me in my loss and for using grief to bring me to a place of hope, healing, and wholeness. In Jesus' Name, Amen.

From Head to Heart:

♥ Are you in denial over your grief? How can you come to terms with your loss and begin to process what has happened? Reach out to a medical professional or trained counselor if needed.

♥ Journaling can be a good way to help process your grief. Either use a paper journal or computer to journal your thoughts and feelings related to your loss.

Day 27

A Time to Mourn

There is a time for everything, and a season for every activity under the heavens: a time to be born and a time to die,...a time to weep and a time to laugh, a time to mourn and a time to dance. Ecclesiastes 3:1, 2a, 4

Scotland is a land of many churches and abbeys, each rich in history with fascinating stories. When I visited Sweetheart Abbey in the Lowland town of New Abbey, I admired the beauty of its ruins. Commissioned by a Scottish noblewoman named Lady Dervorguilla to honor her deceased husband, the church was built in 1275 of dark red sandstone. Its Gothic structure is still imposing and beautiful today.

When her husband, Sir John, died, Lady Dervorguilla had his heart embalmed and placed in a tiny ivory and silver casket. Everywhere she went in life, she carried this small sarcophagus with her. In death, she was buried in Sweetheart Abbey, clutching the box containing her husband's heart.

I admire Lady Dervorguilla's love for her husband, her desire to see him honored, and her tenacity in holding onto his memory. Yet I wonder why she carried his embalmed heart with her everywhere. Perhaps her grief was so great that she spent over twenty years in intense mourning as she held on to the box. Perhaps the little casket was simply a reminder of her beloved husband. Did she think she'd forget him if she let the box go? Maybe his embalmed heart was the only thing she had left of him. Did she feel she would lose her husband all over again if she let go of the box?

In our grief over losing our loved ones, sometimes it's easier to hold onto the pain than to let it go. Grieving is gut-wrenching, but sometimes it is all we have. We hold onto it because to let go of it is like letting go of them.

In Ecclesiastes 3, we read that there is a time for everything. There is a time to weep and a time to mourn. That's entirely appropriate and absolutely necessary. Verse 4 says there is a time to laugh and a time to dance, to get to a healthy place where pain and sorrow are not our constant companions.

Each of us grieves on our own timetable. Take the time you need. But if grief starts to take on a life of its own or begins to define you, stop and ask yourself where you are in the grieving process. Grieving healthily means coming to terms with our loss and realizing that no matter what, we will not forget our loved ones as the memory of them lives in our hearts forever. We can begin to loosen our grip on grief to allow God to begin to heal us. Often a professional counselor or clergy can help us sort through our feelings.

We are wise to let grief take its course until we've worked through the intensity of our loss. While the pain of loss will always be in our hearts, we gain strength as we come to grips with death and step out into life once more. Do the hard, intentional work of grieving until that intense sense of grief has passed. Then address grief when it bubbles up, but don't stay focused on it all the time. Give grief the attention it needs until you can let go of the box.

Dear God, doing the hard work of grieving is exhausting. Thank You for Your supernatural strength that I can call on in times of need. Help me keep a healthy perspective on my sense of loss. I thank You for Your presence as I process my pain and move toward life again. In Jesus' Name, Amen.

From Head to Heart:

♥ In your grief, is there something you are tightly holding onto that has become an obstacle in the course of your healing?

♥ If the answer above is "yes", what can you do to let go of your fear and move forward toward healing?

Day 28

Finding Oasis in the Desert

Blessed are those whose strength is in you, whose hearts are set on pilgrimage. As they pass through the Valley of Baka, they make it a place of springs; the autumn rains also cover it with pools. Psalm 84:5-6

On the journey of grief, we travel through valley after valley. These troughs of despair leave us feeling lonely and despondent. We trudge along as pilgrims in an unfamiliar land, wandering through the desert, feeling parched and desperate for refreshment.

As sojourners in a barren land, we look to the horizon. Is it a mirage or is there really a spring of water on the horizon? Are we delirious or is there really an oasis up ahead?

The Bible says in Psalm 84 that we are pilgrims on a journey. The word "Baka" means weeping. As we walk through the Valley of Weeping, we can find a place of springs, an oasis in our desert, a respite we need as we move through grief.

How do we find this oasis in the midst of the desert? Psalm 84 holds three keys to finding what we need on our journey. The first is in verse 4 where the Bible says "Blessed are those who dwell in your house; they are ever praising you." The key here is the word "dwell". Seeking God's presence through prayer, meditation, music, and reading His word will quench our thirsty souls. Even in our grief, when we're heartbroken over our circumstances, praising God for who He is starts us on the way to healing.

The second key is that God provides us the strength to go on (verses 5-6). Even though our feet are heavy as we stumble along, God walks with us, sometimes carrying us when we are too weak and full of despair. Even though our hearts are heavy, He has not abandoned us. Pray for God's supernatural strength to fill you today.

The last key found in Psalm 84 is in verse 12, "LORD Almighty, blessed is the one who trusts in you." Trusting God who has your very best interests at heart and loves you so much will make a difference in your outlook. While you may have questions in your grief, trust that God will take care of you and that you will begin to heal. Be patient with your progress and trust the One who walks with you.

Open your eyes to see the oasis. Dwell in God's presence. Ask for His strength. Trust that He will provide what you need as He walks with you through the desert.

Dear God, I thank You for walking with me through this Valley of Weeping. Make my pilgrimage a place of springs. Help me seize opportunities for respite, rest, and refreshment. Thank You for Your presence and strength and for being my Jehovah-jireh, my provider. In Jesus' Name, Amen.

From Head to Heart:

- ♥ Read Psalm 84 in its entirety. Ask God for His presence and strength. Trust He will answer you.

\

- ♥ What respite is available to you today? What one thing can you do for yourself to bring rest and refreshment to your mind, body, and soul?

Day 29

Bridge Over Troubled Water

My heart, O God, is steadfast, my heart is steadfast; I will sing and make music. Psalm 57:7

I love the lyrics to Simon and Garfunkel's song entitled "Bridge Over Troubled Water". The words express comforting someone, literally being an emotional bridge over troubled water.

Music has a way of reaching deep into our souls and touching us like nothing else can. Even when we can't express our thoughts and feelings, lyrics can do that for us. When we hear a heart-felt song, we realize we are not alone. We feel connected. It amazes me how often a song can change my mood, particularly from sad to happy.

My brother Logan began playing bass guitar at age 12. Throughout his teenaged years and into his early twenties, he played in rock and roll bands, often with musicians older and more experienced than he. Bass guitar became his passion and he honed his craft over the years through many hours of practice.

As his sister, I was his greatest fan. Many of his bands practiced at our house and I frequently joined them in the basement to listen. After he passed away, listening to those classic rock tunes his bands played helped me feel closer to Logan. The lyrics often swept me back to a time of shared memories with him, transporting me back to a simpler life, a time when I had no idea he would live to be only forty-eight.

For me, music has been a bridge over troubled water with the power to lift me out of a slump and set me on my feet again. Contemporary Christian praise music is often based on words from the Psalms. In the Bible, the Book of Psalms contains many chapters that were intended to be sung, some of which were written by David, the shepherd boy turned king. Often a Psalm begins with wondering where God is in the midst of trouble, only to find at the end, that God is the God who sees, who hears, and who cares.

In Psalm 57, David is on the run from King Saul, who plans to kill him. Saul enters the very cave where David and his men are hiding. God protects David from Saul and later David pens this song of praise to his Lord out of gratitude. David's heart is steadfast, meaning that David completely trusts in God. Psalm 57:7 is a beautiful reminder that when we trust God completely, in whatever circumstances and trials we find ourselves, He will deliver us. We, too, can sing songs of gratitude.

Even in grief, when we focus on God and His love for us, we, too, can experience His presence, helping us to rise above our circumstances, freeing our souls to sing praises to the God who sees us, the God who hears us, and the God who cares for us.

Dear God, I thank You for the Psalms and the connection with the writers of those early songs. The heartfelt words create a bridge within my sorrow to lift me up out of the mire to a place of praise and gratitude. I thank You, not for my circumstances, but in spite of them. You alone are worthy to be praised. In Jesus' Name, Amen.

From Head to Heart:

- ♥ What music can you listen to today that will lift your spirits? Find some Christian songs and hymns that are meaningful to you and listen to them today.

- ♥ Read Psalm 57 in its entirety. Can you relate to David crying out to the Lord in verse 2? Know God's love and faithfulness are for you today (verse 10).

Day 30

Fragrant Memories

But Timothy has just now come to us from you and has brought good news about your faith and love. He has told us that you always have pleasant memories of us and that you long to see us, just as we long to see you. Therefore, brothers and sisters, in all our distress and persecution we were encouraged about you because of your faith. 1 Thessalonians 3:6-7

The sense of smell is closely linked to memory. Capable of evoking powerful memories, a scent transports us back to a particular time and place stored in our memory bank. Even thinking of a particular smell without actually smelling it conjures up memories from long ago.

As we approached the French hillside town of Grasse, our local tour guide shared information about how the perfume industry got its start in Provence many years ago. Grasse has been and still is the perfume capital of France and even the world. Coco Chanel traveled there and had a perfume made just for her. The perfumer, or "Nose", as they are called, made several different versions. Coco chose the fifth version because five was her favorite number. And so Chanel #5 was born.

Just thinking about Chanel #5 and its unique fragrance stirred memories of my mother from my childhood. In a montage of memory-bites that flashed in my mind, I felt sad but strangely comforted as the thought of her scent lingered in my heart as if she were still alive.

As I indulged the flashback, memories of my mother sparingly using her Chanel #5 for church on Sundays and for special occasions paraded through my brain. I recalled seeing her in her younger days, all dressed up in her Southern fashion, wearing a dress, heels, and the string of pearls my dad gave her on their wedding day. She was full of energy and life, very capable and strong. While it is still painful at times to think about her since her death in 2015, I feel comforted by those pleasant memories of her when she had her health and before Alzheimer's disease had taken its toll on her mind. I'm thankful her spirit never wavered during those last years, and in some ways the dementia stripped away the bitterness of life experiences that had threatened to harden her heart. She became once more, the sweet person with a sense of humor everyone loved.

In our key verse today, Timothy brought the apostle Paul greetings from the believers at Thessalonica. Paul and the church members at Thessalonica have good memories of their time together and those memories serve as encouragement to Paul. In our own life, memories of our loved ones may roll over us like waves of grief when we least expect it. The tide of unending love for those who have gone on before us washes up on the beaches of our souls, again and again. Let the love those good memories hold wash you clean, taking the sadness away as it ebbs and flows and replace the tears with God's encouragement, comfort, and peace.

Dear God, thank You for the triggers that evoke memories of our loved ones. May we hold onto the good memories and let go of the painful ones. May we find comfort in Your peace and presence. In Jesus' Name, Amen.

From Head to Heart:

♥ Has a scent or fragrance evoked a memory of your loved one? What was the scent and what memory did it trigger?

♥ The next time a good memory of your loved one is triggered, try sitting with that memory and allowing it to comfort you. Spending appropriate time in our grief can aid us in the healing process.

Day 31

On Eagles' Wings

He gives strength to the weary and increases the power of the weak. Even youths grow tired and weary, and young men stumble and fall; but those who hope in the LORD will renew their strength. They will soar on wings like eagles; they will run and not grow weary, they will walk and not be faint.
Isaiah 40:29-31

I was recently in Portland, Oregon, and drove over to the coast. Cannon Beach is a quaint, though touristy, beach town with a plethora of shops and art galleries. While meandering through this charming hamlet was fun, I enjoyed the walk down to the beach to Haystack Rock. This enormous rock sits on the edge of the shore and is indeed shaped like a haystack. Hundreds of seagulls were flying around the rock, perching there for a while before taking off again over the water and sand.

As I watched the gulls fly overhead, I was reminded of a verse in Scripture found in Isaiah, chapter 40: "They will soar on wings like eagles; they will run and not grow weary, they will walk and not be faint." Although a seagull is a far cry from a majestic eagle, both birds expend much energy flapping their wings as they take off. When they catch a thermal, they can stop beating their wings and just glide.

Seeing all of those seagulls soar on the air currents, seemingly floating there, reminded me that there are many times in our lives when we, like the people mentioned in Isaiah, are tired and weary. We stumble and fall. When we lose someone we love, life is overwhelming and requires a great amount of physical and emotional energy. Viewing our journey from the ground can be discouraging. But rising above it on "eagles' wings", catching a thermal and soaring above our difficulties, gives us a new perspective. When we wait on the Lord, when we put our hope and our trust in Him, He gives us the strength we need to overcome the obstacles in our path. He truly does increase the power of the weak. We will run and not grow weary. We will walk and not be faint.

Just watching the birds fly overhead gave a lift to my spirit and reminded me that God does care about me and the details of my life. How freeing it was to watch those seagulls flap their wings and fly, wafting onward with the wind beneath them. And for a few moments, I, too, was soaring with them.

Dear God, I thank You for moments of grace in the midst of life's difficulties. Thank You for the beauty of Your creation, for beaches and birds. I pray for strength when I'm weary and for Your power when I am weak. Thank You for the energy to carry on, to fly on wings like eagles, to run and not grow weary, to walk and not be faint. In Jesus' Name, Amen.

From Head to Heart:

- ♥ What activity do you enjoy? Make plans now to do one thing to give you respite from your grief.

- ♥ Sometimes it takes stopping, looking, and listening to God's spirit within us to see a new perspective. Make it a practice to "stop and smell the roses", to notice your surroundings, and to find joy and meaning in the everyday.

Day 32

No Room at the Inn

So Joseph also went up from the town of Nazareth in Galilee to Judea, to Bethlehem the town of David, because he belonged to the house and line of David. He went there to register with Mary, who was pledged to be married to him and was expecting a child. While they were there, the time came for the baby to be born, and she gave birth to her first-born, a son. She wrapped him in cloths and placed him in a manger, because there was no room for them in the inn. Luke 2:4-7*

"It's the most wonderful time of the year!" At least these were the words of the Christmas song I was hearing as it played on my laptop. I was listening to it just to get me in the mood for the holidays. Christmas is the time we celebrate the birth of Jesus and spend time with family and friends. But does it feel like the most wonderful time of the year to you?

The holidays can be a lonely and depressing time for many. The well-wishes of "Merry Christmas" can strike sorrow in the hearts of those of us who grieve. The contrast of the holiday celebrations and all the hype our culture attaches to them is stark against the sadness in our hearts over the loss of someone we love. We know we have to endure the holidays with an empty place at the table.

On the night of Jesus' birth, Mary and Joseph arrived in Bethlehem after a long and tiring journey. Plodding through the town, they looked for a place to stay for the night. Imagine their frustration and sheer exhaustion as they trudged from house to house. No one had a room for them. No one seemed to care. At last, they were offered a room…but in a dirty, smelly stable. No private room here as they shared it with the innkeeper's animals. How tired and weary Mary must have been.

Are you tired and weary, too? Are you dreading the holidays? Are you going through the motions just to get to January? You are not alone. The holidays are difficult when someone we love is not there. We feel their absence most acutely when everyone else is celebrating. The happiness of others accentuates our sorrow.

How do you get through this challenging holiday and other special occasions? Acknowledge to yourself and even to those closest to you that the holidays are difficult for you. Try to think ahead to the holiday gatherings and determine what will be most difficult. What holiday traditions do you hold? Which ones will be especially painful for you? What change can you make that will bring you less pain? For example, if everyone has assigned seats at the Christmas dinner table, then maybe you mix up the seating and remove one place. Or conversely, maybe you leave the place setting so they are not forgotten. Do what works for you.

Every year at Christmas when we gathered at my parents' house, Mom would hang up our stockings by the fireplace. These were the stockings of our childhood which she had sewn for us. After my brother passed away, Mom continued to hang up his stocking. Although it remained empty, his stocking hanging from the mantle was a sweet reminder that he was still a part of our family.

Think about your Christmas traditions. Tweak them if you need to, or consider starting new ones. Spend time with those who understand your grief. Do what is comforting to you. Acknowledge that the holidays are difficult but know you will get through them. Know that the baby Jesus born that holy night grew up to suffer loneliness and sorrow, too. He came down from heaven to a humble stable so that you might know Him. Let Him comfort you with His presence and His peace. He loves you so.

Dear God, thank You for coming from heaven to be born in a lowly stable that holy night. Even though there was no room at the inn for You, You always have room for me. Fill me with Your presence. Comfort me with Your peace. In Jesus' Name, Amen.

From Head to Heart:

- ♥ Dreading upcoming holidays and special occasions is normal when you are grieving. Being proactive can take away some of the tension. What one thing can you plan today to make it easier for you?

- ♥ Whose help can you enlist to make the next occasion more tolerable?

Day 33

A Necessary Remembrance

I thank my God every time I remember you. Philippians 1:3

Every family has its traditions. Some may have many customs they practice. Others may have just a few. When I was growing up, one of my family's traditions was to celebrate each other's birthdays by going out to dinner. Since my mother cooked every night, going out to dinner was something special and unusual. I'm sure my mom enjoyed a break from the routine of cooking. We, as children, loved to go to our favorite all-you-can-eat seafood restaurant. My parents loved it because children under twelve ate for free.

As we got older, we were allowed to choose other restaurants. I remember on one birthday, I selected a nice Chinese restaurant. Back in the day, this would have been one of my first forays into ethnic cuisine. I loved it. I can't say my mom did. But regardless of where we ate or whose birthday it was, my dad always paid the bill, even on his own birthday and even when we were grown.

Today is my father's birthday. There will be no dinners out, no birthday cake or candles, no presents, visits, or phone calls. He passed away over seven years ago. Having a birthday close to Christmas, he often received combined birthday and Christmas gifts. He never complained about sharing his birthday with Jesus. And he also never complained about the fruitcake I often bought him for his birthday. He was the only person I knew who actually liked fruitcake!

Today I feel sad. Even though it's been a few years since my dad passed away, my grief today has caught me unawares. Surprised by the intensity of my sense of loss, I let it flow over me. I sit in silence and remember. I remember his last days of struggle and suffering and am glad he is in heaven with Jesus where there are no more tears, pain, or death. I remember his life, how hard he worked to provide for his family. I remember his intelligence, how he knew so much about so many things. I remember his character, how he was honest and filled with integrity. He was the kind of person who never met a stranger. I remember the good times and the bad. Although he wasn't perfect, he was still my dad. I loved him and still do. I miss him.

Birthdays are an occasion to remember and honor those who are still living. But when celebrating another year isn't possible, birthdays can be a day to remember, a necessary remembrance that brings healing to our souls as we continue down the path of grief.

Although our key verse was written to the church at Philippi, today I read these words in remembrance of my dad, who lived and loved until he left his frail body to live with Jesus. May we not forget those who have passed on before us. They will forever live in our hearts.

Dear God, today I remember someone dear to me that has passed from this life to the next. Although my mind is filled with sadness over my loss, my heart is full of memories and love. Use this time to allow grief to do its work in my life to bring me to a place of healing. In Jesus' Name, Amen.

From Head to Heart:

♥ What family traditions do you celebrate? Which ones are no longer celebrated? Which one is your favorite? Why?

♥ What can you do to remember loved ones, either today or on their birthday?

Day 34

An Altar of Remembrance

"Then come, let us go up to Bethel, where I will build an altar to God, who answered me in the day of my distress and who has been with me wherever I have gone." Genesis 35:3

On a trip to the Lowlands of Scotland, I visited several abbeys. Located in New Abbey along the banks of the River Pow, Sweetheart Abbey is a testament of a woman's love for her husband. Lady Dervorguilla of Galloway commissioned the abbey to be built of local, red sandstone and named it Dulce Cor (Latin for "sweet heart") in memory of her husband, John Balliol. Completed in 1275, the beautiful abbey housed Cistercian monks until 1610. Although the abbey's roof and several walls are missing, it still stands tall for this lady's everlasting love.

In biblical times, altars of stones stacked one on top of another were created to remember personal encounters with God or to honor God's acts of faithfulness. In the book of Genesis, Jacob is pursued by his brother Esau, who plans to kill him. During his flight from danger, Jacob encounters God through a dream (Genesis 28:13-17). In today's key verse, Jacob plans to build an altar of stone to honor God and commemorate this pivotal event in his life.

In our culture today, stone altars aren't commonplace. The stacks of stones I often see are markers along hiking trails. Unlike Lady Dervorguilla, most of us can't afford to build huge structures as monuments to our loved ones. Yet we can commemorate our loved ones' lives in other, less massive, ways. Displaying their prized possessions in our home reminds us of them and honors them by honoring their belongings. Hanging framed photos of them in our home helps remind us they are not forgotten. Contributing financially to a cause dear to them helps memorialize our loved ones. There are many other ways to remember our loved ones, each one as unique as they were.

I admire Lady Dervorguilla's love for her husband and her desire to honor him. In the process, she built a beautiful abbey that lives on long after their time on earth. Our remembrances may or may not last for centuries, but we can build testaments to our loved ones' lives in ways that bring them honor. In the process, we will find comfort for ourselves. Like Jacob who built an altar to God, we too can remember God's encounter with us as we walk our journey of grief.

Dear God, I thank You for Your unending faithfulness to me. I thank You for my loved ones' lives. Show me how to best honor their memory. In Jesus' Name, Amen.

From Head to Heart:

- ♥ How have you honored the memory of your loved one? What ways can you do that?

- ♥ God is faithful to us. He promises to never leave us (Hebrews 13:5). As He walks with you in your grief journey, in what ways can you honor Him?

Day 35

Numbering Our Days

Teach us to number our days, that we may gain a heart of wisdom. Psalm 90:12

Today is my birthday. Not one of those milestone birthdays. Just one in between. I'm not as excited about my birthdays like I was when I was kid, eagerly awaiting parties and presents. But this day is still my special day. Birthdays are days to celebrate life and to anticipate many more years to come.

My brother Logan was just shy of his 49th birthday when he died suddenly of a massive heart attack. Family members and friends gathered on his special day to memorialize his "almost" birthday at his favorite restaurant, but our celebration was markedly different that year. To celebrate what would have been is bittersweet at best. To remember what will never be is agonizing in the very least. Being together, however, did help bring a small bit of closure to our tender and aching hearts.

Psalm 90:12 says "Teach us to number our days, that we may gain a heart of wisdom." Life is short. We don't know how many days or years we have left. Our "death day" is unknown to us. God's Word tells us to consider the shortness of our days, which are only shadows of life eternal. Ponder what you want the rest of your life to be like. Gain God's heart of wisdom through prayer and reading His Word so the choices you make today will positively impact the rest of your days. Matthew 6:33 tells us to seek His kingdom and His righteousness first. Determine your values and priorities and be true to them. Live a life well-lived.

For those of us who have lost loved ones, our birthdays, as well as theirs, are difficult days. Although these times are bittersweet as we recall birthdays that are gone forever, try to live in the present. Dwelling on the past or being anxious for the future is futile. Thinking of what might have been or what will never be is depressing. Commemorate these special days in ways that are both meaningful and healing. Spend time with those who matter most to you. Spend time with the God who loves you. Make each day count. Life is too short not to.

Dear God, I know You hold my days in Your hands. I know not how long I have left on this earth, so please give me a heart of wisdom so I can live each day to the fullest. Help me to seek You first in all I do. May my life be a celebration to Your glory every day. In Jesus' Name, Amen.

From Head to Heart:

♥ How can you commemorate your loved one's birthday or other special occasion? Is there a new tradition you can start? Are there friends and family to share that occasion with in order to ease your pain?

♥ How can you make today count? Is there something you've been putting off that needs to be done? Alternatively, can you carve out time today to read God's Word and pray?

Day 36

Orphaned

"In my Father's house are many rooms; if it were not so, I would have told you. I am going there to prepare a place for you." John 14:2*

Mother's Day and Father's Day are what I refer to as "Hallmark holidays". While it sometimes felt like a command performance to send flowers or fruit, or to visit my parents, I believe that we should honor our parents *every* day by telling and showing them our gratitude. The Bible even commands us to honor our fathers and mothers (Exodus 20:12). It's not optional!

This most recent of Mother's Days was unexpectedly difficult. Being the first Mother's Day since my mom passed away, this occasion was a reminder to me that she was no longer here. Advertisements imploring me to buy that special gift for my mother only served to rub salt into the gaping wound.

I know I'm not alone. I have several friends who have lost their moms over the last few months. This day that was supposed to be a time of celebration was more difficult than they expected, too.

As the advertisements gear up for Father's Day, I'm not looking forward to this particular occasion either. Although it's been over seven years since my dad passed away, Father's Day is not an opportunity for me to celebrate. As the years since his death come and go, I am beginning to turn my "mourning into dancing" as I know my dad is in heaven. I can be thankful for his life. In the future, I know I'll get to the same place with Mom and Mother's Day. Time doesn't necessarily heal all wounds, but it can often take the edge off the pain.

Although I'm all grown-up with children of my own, having lost both parents I often feel like an orphan with no home to go to, no parental advice to call upon, and no feelings of a "safety net". It's just me. Except I'm the one providing a home base for my now-grown children who still look to Mom for advice in navigating the world. I'm *their* safety net.

It's a bit scary to be "orphaned". Not only are there feelings of abandonment, but there's this in-your-face idea of your own mortality. Thankfully, I have a deeper sense of home. In John 14:2, Jesus says, "In my Father's house are many rooms; if it were not so, I would have told you. I am going there to prepare a place for you." My home isn't here on this earth. It's an eternal home in heaven with Jesus. And when I arrive in heaven, both my parents and my brother Logan will be waiting to welcome me home.

Dear God, I know I'm just passing through life here on earth on the way to my eternal home with You. Until You take me home, may I bring glory to You as I love and honor those in my life with the grace that comes from You. In Jesus' Name, Amen.

From Head to Heart:

- ♥ How are certain significant days difficult for you? What can you do in advance to prepare yourself for the next one?

- ♥ Do you know the hope of heaven? If not, become a child of God today. Ask Jesus into your heart by asking His forgiveness for your wrongdoings. None of us are perfect and we each have done deeds or said words that are hurtful. Trust that His sacrificial death on the cross was sufficient to pay for your sins. Enter into a personal relationship with Jesus by trusting Him to be your Savior and Lord.

Day 37

Acceptance

Be strong and courageous. Do not be afraid or terrified because of them, for the LORD your God goes with you; he will never leave you nor forsake you. Deuteronomy 31:6

We often hear about the stages of grief. While grief is not neat and orderly and doesn't fall into categories easily, it is important to understand the different facets of grief. Acceptance is often the most difficult stage and it's challenging to grasp what it means to accept the loss. Let's start by thinking about what acceptance is not. Accepting the fact that our loved ones are gone is not the same as saying it is okay they are gone or that we are moving on and forgetting them. Acceptance is not finishing up our grief work and saying we're done.

Accepting our loss means acknowledging our loved one is gone. It means deciding we are going to go on living in spite of our loss. It means knowing that life is different now and we must find that new normal. Acceptance is choosing to process our grief, not run from it. Intense grief may still bubble up from time to time, and that's okay. We will deal with it when it does and then get back to living.

There may be guilt associated with acceptance. We feel we are betraying our loved ones if we decide we're moving on without them. The reality is that they would want us to move forward. We can do so while holding the memories of them in our hearts.

Acceptance is a healthy way of dealing with loss. It may take some time to get there, so be patient with yourself. You will know you have arrived at acceptance when you are no longer emotionally paralyzed. The pain of the loss may not have lessened, but the resolve to go on living in spite of it draws you down the path of healing.

Grief is a journey, not a destination. Acceptance is saying we're not stopped on the road of grief, stuck in a ditch, but we are continually walking forward, making progress, even if it is baby steps at a time. Deciding to move forward is a healthy response to our pain. It means we plan to face our new life head-on, even though we don't know what lies ahead. But God does.

In Deuteronomy 31:6, as he stands on the edge of the Promised Land, Moses tells the people of Israel to take the land God has promised them and He will give them victory over the obstacles they will encounter. Moses tells them to be strong and courageous because the Lord goes with them. You, too, can be strong and brave because God goes with you. He has a plan for your life and you need not be afraid. He knows the goodness of His promises and any obstacles you will encounter. He walks with you into the future.

You don't have to be stuck in your grief. Remember that grief is only a journey. The destination is a place of wholeness and healing, a clearing in the woods where we find respite for our souls, and a habitat of peace, love, and yes, even joy. Walk beside the Savior. You are not alone.

Dear God, You know my heart and You see my struggles. Accepting my loss is necessary for me to move forward in my grief to a place of hope and healing. Give me the strength to decide to accept that my loved one is gone and for me to go on living. Give me the courage to walk into the future with You by my side. In Jesus' Name, Amen.

From Head to Heart:

♥ Do you feel guilty when you think about accepting your loss? How can you move forward while remembering your loved ones and not forgetting them?

♥ What can you do today to begin to accept your loss? What decisions can you make that will spur you on toward healing?

Day 38

Mourning to Dancing

You turned my wailing into dancing; you removed my sackcloth and clothed me with joy, that my heart may sing your praises and not be silent. LORD my God, I will praise you forever. Psalm 30:11-12

Grief is a journey, not a destination. Camping out in the tent of grief is not a healthy option and only serves to lengthen the difficult task of healing. Likewise, avoiding feelings of loss or dulling pain through unhealthy pursuits only stalls the healing and poisons our relationships.

When we move through grief, rather than avoiding it or marinating in it, we find strength to continue our journey of healing. Moving through grief means consciously staying in touch with our thoughts and feelings. Gently correcting rogue thoughts that hold us captive, we gain confidence in our ability to stay the course in healing. Grieving is not avoiding

147

our feelings but rather embracing them as a means to explore, learn, and grow. Pain is never wasted when we dance with our Savior. No sorrow is too great for Him. Loss through death has much to teach us about life. Our pain does have a purpose, whether to grow us into who we are meant to be or to extend comfort to someone similarly grieving. Often, we experience both.

Grieving well doesn't mean turning to unhealthy ways to dull our pain or to escape. There is no other way except through our pain. Detours to anesthetize our pain will only prolong it. Grief waits patiently until we are ready to deal with it. Losses, like open wounds, fester and ooze poisonous thoughts and feelings into our relationships. The sooner we move toward healing, the healthier we will be. We'll still carry the scar and for a while, the scab, but the wound will be healing.

While it may last a long time, at some point the intensity of loss will diminish, allowing us to live again. Allowing God to walk with us on our journey of grief can bring us peace and joy. Embracing the wound in the presence of the One who heals creates space for healing. God alone can turn our mourning into dancing, our sorrow into joy, our despair into peace. Our wounded spirits can dance again, free from suffering. We'll find we are praising Him for who He is and for His great love for us. We will look back and realize He walked beside us on our journey of grief. And as we turn towards Him, we will know He is not only with us in the journey, He is our destination and our hope.

Dear God, grief is a journey, an unwanted one but a necessary one to find healing. Thank You for turning my mourning into dancing. I praise You for the ways You continue to care for me. Thank You for bringing me thus far and I trust You to see my healing through to completion. In Jesus' Name, Amen.

From Head to Heart:

- ♥ How have you stalled grieving by either avoiding it or by dulling its pain? What can you do to change that approach?

- ♥ How has Jesus walked with you on your journey of grief? Give thanks and praise Him for the specific ways you have felt His presence and peace.

Day 39

Wounded Healer

Many Jews had come to Martha and Mary to comfort them in the loss of their brother. John 11:19

In John 11, we learn that Lazarus, a friend of Jesus and the brother of Martha and Mary, had died. In Biblical times, the Jews usually buried their dead on the day they passed away. Their customs dictated that mourners show their respect for the bereaved on the third day. So when many mourners from Jerusalem came to comfort Martha and Mary on the third day after Lazarus' death, they must have walked roughly two miles to Bethany.

Jesus arrived in Bethany on the fourth day. Both Martha and Mary were beside themselves with grief. They knew that if Jesus had been there, Lazarus would not have died. But Jesus had other plans. He delayed coming to Bethany so he could raise Lazarus from the dead. It was a true miracle for all to see so that they might put their faith in Jesus.

I wonder what would have happened if there were no rules or customs that required the Jews from Jerusalem to officially grieve with Martha and Mary. Many scholars believe that Lazarus, Martha, and Mary were from a prominent, well-to-do family. I wonder, too, if the people would have walked that far if Martha and Mary had been poor or just ordinary members of society. Perhaps their suffering would have been dismissed. Or perhaps only a few would have walked the distance to Bethany.

Fast forward to our own time and culture. When we hear of friends losing a family member, what do we do to help them? Do we believe that they will get over it soon enough without our assistance? Are we so busy with our own lives that we can't pause to comfort those who mourn?

Often, experiencing a particular event gives us the capacity to understand a similar event in someone else's life. Losing someone you love is heart-breaking and gut-wrenching. When we encounter a friend or even a family member who doesn't "get it", keep in mind that it isn't that they don't care. They just don't realize how painful it is.

When we mourn our own losses well, we can then extend love and comfort to others who have experienced similar losses. We can walk alongside them in their own grief journey as we offer hope and healing. Whether we walk two miles like the Jerusalem mourners or drive many miles to be with someone in need, we'll discover comfort for ourselves, too, as we become travelers together in this journey of life and loss.

Dear God, I thank You that You are always with me, even when those around me don't understand my pain. May I care for those who need Your healing touch, just as You care for me. In Jesus' Name, Amen.

From Head to Heart:

- ♥ To whom can you be a "wounded healer" today? Take a first step towards comforting someone else with the same comfort you have received yourself.

- ♥ How can you offer grace and forgiveness to someone who doesn't understand your own sense of loss?

Day 40

Carpe Diem

LORD, what are human beings that you care for them, mere mortals that you think of them? They are like a breath; their days are like a fleeting shadow. Psalm 144:3-4

Life is short; it seems to fly by at warp speed. How many of us consider the brevity of our days? I'm sure I didn't until my 48-year-old brother Logan suddenly passed away. Life quickly took on new meaning for me.

In Psalm 144, David realizes how fleeting life is. He compares life to a mere shadow cast by the shining sun. In the heat of the day, shadows lengthen and quickly fade. Life on earth is also short. What life lessons can these evanescent shadows teach us?

For those of us who mourn the loss of someone we love, we understand how brief life is. Living in the present moment is difficult at best. The future seems out of reach. Part of my healing process has been to realize how quickly life on earth can end and the importance of "carpe diem". Seize the day. Make the most of every minute.

Do you have a bucket list? Are there dreams, goals, and activities on that list that need tending to before it's too late? On my bucket list, there are many goals I'd like to accomplish and places I'd like to travel to. I'm so thankful that in the years since Logan passed away, I've accomplished many things on my list. I still have lots of items untouched, but I'm making progress. And as I do, I find healing.

Another lesson taught to me by the fleeting shadows of life is the importance of relationships. Never take for granted the opportunity to spend time with those you love. Make the most of the time you have with family and friends before it's too late.

The first part of Ecclesiastes 11:8 says "However many years anyone may live, let them enjoy them all." We don't know how much time each of us has left on planet earth. Seize the day! Enjoy life to the fullest. Find joy in the goodness of the Lord. Look for joy even in small, everyday things. When you do, you will discover healing in each of those moments.

Dear God, thank You for the opportunities You give me each and every day. Help me to seize each day and make the most of my time here on earth. May I live, love, and honor You with all that I do. In Jesus' Name, Amen.

From Head to Heart:

♥ "Seizing the day" may feel overwhelming. Start small. Find one moment of joy today.

♥ What is one item on your bucket list that you most want to accomplish? What can you do today to start making that happen?

What's Next?

It is my hope and prayer that as you travel your journey of grief this devotional book has helped you in the healing process. I pray you will know you are not alone, that others, like me, are also traveling alongside you on this journey. But more importantly, I pray you will feel the Lord's presence and experience His love and comfort.

Below are some of the truths I discovered when losing my brother as well as both my parents in a short span of just under seven years. May these truths draw you nearer to God as you move toward healing.

1 - The first step toward healing from grief is recognizing and admitting you are grieving.

2 - Grieving is gut-wrenching, but sometimes that is all you feel you have. Letting go of it is like letting go of your loved one. But in the letting go, there is healing.

3 - You have to grieve, cry, be overtaken by your grief, and otherwise experience it in order to discover healing. Ignoring your grief will not bring the gifts of healing, such as compassion, peace, a sense of aliveness and freedom, and yes, even a sense of joy.

4 - Face your fear by stepping out of your comfort zone over and over, knowing Jesus is with you wherever you go and whatever you do.

5 - God weaves the painful threads of our lives into a fabric that is truly beautiful. Taking the heartache, He transforms it into something glorious for Him and something good for us. Our pain serves a purpose.

6 - Grief is a journey, not a destination. Grief doesn't define you; it's just the path you're on right now.

Blessings to you, my friend and fellow traveler.

LORD my God, I called to you for help, and you healed me…
You turned my wailing into dancing;
you removed my sackcloth and clothed me with joy,
that my heart may sing your praises and not be silent.
LORD my God, I will praise you forever.
Psalm 30: 2, 11-12

Author's Note

Thank you for reading this book. I hope it was helpful. I love hearing from my readers. You can reach me via private email at *dawn@dawndailey.org*.

My prayer is that those who need this devotional book on grief will find it. Your review will ensure that others' search for a grief book will lead them to this one. If you are so inclined, please take a moment to write a review on Amazon.com. I appreciate your support so much.

I regularly write and post inspirational stories on my website. View them at *https://dawndailey.org/blog-on-life-faith-and-grief.html*. Feel free to subscribe to these devotional-style blog posts so you can receive them as an email directly in your in-box. Sign up at *https://dawndailey.org/about-ussubscribe.html*.

If you are grieving the loss of an adult sibling or know someone who is, please check out my book entitled *Losing Logan: Grieving the Death of an Adult Sibling*. Purchase a copy today at *https://www.amazon.com/dp/149594476X* or order it through any independent bookseller.

Thank you so much. May the Lord continue to walk with you on your journey of grief.

Made in the USA
Middletown, DE
26 January 2022

59663771R00102